SIMPLE
TALKS
ON THE
TABERNACLE

kregel
PUBLICATIONS

Grand Rapids, MI 49501

Simple Talks on the Tabernacle, by D. H. Dolman. © 1993 by Kregel Publications, a division of Kregel, Inc., P.O. Box 2607, Grand Rapids, MI 49501. All rights reserved.

Cover design: Alan G. Hartman

Library of Congress Cataloging-in-Publication Data

Dolman, D. H.

Simple talks on the tabernacle / by D. H. Dolman.
    p.   cm.
  Previously published: 1985.
    1. Tabernacle—Typology—Sermons. 2. Sermons, English. I. Title.
BS680.T32D65   1993   222'.1064—dc20   92-39335
                                                CIP

ISBN 0-8254-2457-7 (pbk.)

      1 2 3 4 5 Printing / Year 97 96 95 94 93

Printed in the United States of America

CONTENTS

LIST OF ILLUSTRATIONS

PUBLISHER'S PREFACE

Why study the Tabernacle and its furnishings? Dr. D. H. Dolman's *Simple Talks on the Tabernacle* is a clear and concise explanation of the construction and significance of the Tabernacle which provides a positive answer to that question. By relating the teaching of the Old Testament to the New, it presents readers with a clear-cut and carefully applied typology. As Dr. Cyril Barber says in his book, *The Minister's Library*, this work is "A devout, reverent study of the typology of the Tabernacle."

It is a great pleasure for Kregel Publications to make this book available to a new generation of Bible students.

FOREWORD

Within that awful volume lies
The mystery of mysteries!
Happiest they of human race,
To whom God has granted grace
To read, to fear, to hope, to pray,
To lift the latch and force the way;
And better had they ne'er been born,
Who read to doubt, or read to scorn.

In these memorable lines, Sir Walter Scott writes of the value (as well as the responsibility) of understanding what God has chosen to reveal to man in the pages of Holy Writ. One of these mysteries is the incarnation of the Lord Jesus Christ. The Apostle John links the Old Testament with the New when he says, "And the Word [Christ] became flesh, and *tabernacled* among us, and we beheld His glory, glory as of the only begotten of the Father, full of grace and truth" (John 1:14).

This certainly is a great mystery, and for its unfolding we must look back to Exodus, a book of redemption and worship, as well as forward to the teaching of the superiority of Christ in the Book of Hebrews. Without an understanding of the former we will be unable to fully appreciate what is recorded for us in the latter.

In years gone by, the study of the Old Testament was the consuming passion of men and women who believed with Augustine that "The New Testament lies hidden in the Old, and the Old [Testament] is made plain in the New." They knew they could not fully understand the teaching of Christ and the apostles without first mastering the writings of Moses and the prophets. Now, however, it would be difficult for anyone to find in a bookstore a competent explanation of the meaning and significance of the Tabernacle and its furnishings.

The need, therefore, to reprint a competent work on the symbolism and theology of the Tabernacle is no longer an option; it is now a necessity.

The work presently before the reader, Dirk Dolman's *Simple Talks on the Tabernacle*, provides students of the Word with a rare combination of good exposition and the application of devotional truth latent in Israel's sanctuary and worship. It reveals Christ in the relative unattractiveness (to the natural eye) of His humanity as well as the significance of His work.

It has rightly been said that our study of the Scriptures should lead us to worship. As we contemplate the mysteries of Christ contained in the Old Testament, our study should enrich our understanding of the teaching of the Gospel spelled out in greater detail in the New Testament. The result should be praise and adoration, and gratitude issuing in loving service.

Cyril J. Barber
Author, *The Minister's Library*

INTRODUCTION

WE ARE living in an age when the historical, archæological, philological study of the Holy Scriptures is
being carried on with the greatest eagerness, and with
better equipment and more abundant material than at
any previous period in the history of the Church. It is
producing a vast and important literature, and surely
all who love the Word of God must welcome the fruits
of such investigation, and be grateful for a more com-
prehensive knowledge of the historical background of
Biblical events and a more accurate understanding of
the languages in which our Testaments were originally
written.

Yet there is a great danger that in the constant
search for the grammatical and historical meaning of
the records of the Holy Scriptures the deeper, more
spiritual truths of these passages will be ignored, or
at least be given a place of undeserved subordination.
That this is a real danger today is shown by the fact,
which none can dispute, that the literature now appearing relating to historical and archæological matters
relating to the Word of God is vast, important, the
result of years of careful study on the part of distin-
guished scholars, while, on the other hand, the literature which attempts, with equal soundness of learning,
to bring out the great spiritual teachings of the Word
of Truth is for the most part superficial, ephemeral,

more or less sensational, and does not commend itself to our new generation. One reason for this is that men who give themselves day and night to meditation upon the deeper, spiritual truths of the Word, are growing, it seems, increasingly rare.

This book, by my dear friend Dr. Dolman, is a welcome exception to the general trend of Biblical literature today—a devout study of the inner meaning of one of the greatest objects of divinely designed typical meaning in all Scriptures—the Tabernacle. For one to be adequately equipped for discovering the precious treasures the Spirit of God has deposited for our enrichment in the extended portions of the Word devoted to this subject three qualifications are necessary: one must give years of careful study and meditation to the subject itself; one must ever desire to make Christ central in all his thinking; and, one must know a life of true holiness. These three qualifications Dr. Dolman has, in a superlative way. I know of no one today whose own saintly life and love for the Word would quite qualify him for attempting such a work as this, as Dr. Dolman.

Beautiful buildings are necessary to be appreciated— but it is the bread on the table that feeds our souls. Historical study of the Scriptures serves many important purposes; but it is Christ in the Word who nourishes our souls. The entire Christian Church will be grateful to Dr. Dolman for setting before us so rich a feast of the precious, sanctifying, strengthening truths of this portion of the Bread of God.

WILBUR M. SMITH

The Encampment of BENJAMIN, EPHRAIM, and MANASSEH

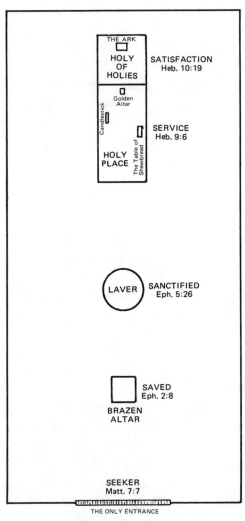

The Encampment of SIMEON, REUBEN, and GAD

The Encampment of ASHER, DAN, and NAPHTALI

MOSES, AARON AND HIS SONS

The Encampment of ZEBULUN, JUDAH, and ISSACHAR

Diagram of Tabernacle with Position of Tribes

AUTHOR'S PREFACE

3. Thou art the fairest among the children of men.
—Psalm 45: 3

FOR MANY years it has been my privilege to teach Jewish young men the way of salvation. Naturally I began by showing them Christ in the Old Testament, how our heavenly Father began to teach His young children in object lessons and how their Messiah was foreshadowed in type and prophecy.

Modern Theology has no room for the study of types. I found that my Bible readings on the tabernacle, a type of Christ and His Church, were greatly blessed to many of God's children in different parts of the States.

The pleasant, quiet time I spent in the hospitable home of my friends, Dr. W. Newell and his kind sister, gave me a welcome opportunity to study once more the teaching of the tabernacle and to write my notes down in book form.

The above words came fresh in my mind in writing. They were often used by my beloved father, when he led his children to the throne of grace in family worship. If they find an echo in the hearts of the readers I shall be deeply thankful.

The Jewish form of worship is well worthy of the study of Christian theologians. It is not the object of this book. It contains only simple heart-to-heart talks to God's children about our precious Redeemer and how we can follow and serve Him best in our daily lives.

I am deeply grateful to my friend Dr. Wilbur M. Smith in giving me his valuable time in carefully perusing the manuscript and commending it in his introduction.

May Saint Paul's prayer (Gal. 5: 19) that Christ be formed in us be heard so that we may not be ashamed at His coming!

D.H.D.

1

HANGINGS OF FINE TWINED LINEN

9. Thou shalt make the court of the tabernacle: for the *south side* there shall be *hangings for the court of fine twined linen of an hundred cubits long.*

10. And the twenty *pillars* and their twenty sockets shall be of brass; the *hooks* of the pillars and their *fillets* shall be of *silver.*

11. And likewise *for the north side* in length there shall be hangings of *an hundred cubits long,* and his twenty pillars and their twenty sockets of brass; the hooks of the pillars and their fillets of silver.

12. And for the breadth of the court *on the west side* shall be hangings of *fifty cubits*: their *pillars ten,* and their *sockets ten.*

13. And the breadth of the court *on the east side eastward* shall be *fifty cubits.*

14. The hangings of one side of the gate shall be *fifteen* cubits: their *pillars three,* and their sockets three.

15. And on the other side shall be hangings fifteen cubits: their *pillars three* and their *sockets three.*—EXODUS 27: 9-15

"WHAT must I do to be saved?" (Acts 16: 30). The jailer's question was no new one. From the very beginning it has risen from hearts which were burdened by their sins. Sin separates from God. There is a wide gulf between sinful man and a holy God. How can this broken communion be restored? Throughout the ages the cry of the soul convicted of sin has been: "What must I do to be saved?" The answer can only be the one Saint Paul gave to the jailer—not by doing, but by believing. "Believe on the Lord Jesus Christ and thou shalt be saved."

The tabernacle was intended to show the believing Israelite the way to restored communion, the way into the sanctuary, the way to the throne, the way to the Father's heart. There is only one way. Our Lord says: "I am the way, the truth, and the life: no man cometh unto the Father, but by me" (John 14: 6). It is clear, therefore, that when we study together the tabernacle, our blessed Lord is the subject of our studies. The tabernacle, its vessels and implements, all speak to us of the Lord Jesus.

But again, there is a close union between our Lord and His Church—I mean those who by regeneration have become members of His body. He is the head; we are the members of His body. Head and body belong together; you cannot separate them. If you do, life would be extinct. It is clear, therefore, that tabernacle and Israel belong together, and it follows that the tabernacle is not only a type of Christ, but also a type of His body, the Church, whose head is Christ. Saint Paul's greatest desire was to know Christ and the power of His resurrection. May this be the deepest longing of our hearts as we reverently study the tabernacle as a type of Christ and what He wants His followers to be.

"Let them make me a sanctuary; that *I may dwell* among them" (Exod. 25: 8). What a wonderful condescension; how the hearts of the people must have thrilled with joy! Not only should God's presence go with them, but He actually promised to dwell amongst them. The tabernacle was to be made according to the pattern Moses had seen in the mount, unto the most minute details.

The tabernacle had to be placed in a court which was to be separated from the desert by curtains, hanging from pillars, and to be entered by a wide gate.

The court was to be an hundred cubits long and fifty broad. The cubit is the length of the forearm; and most Bible students agree that the average length of the forearm is eighteen inches, which would make the length of the court fifty yards and its breadth twenty-five yards. The boundary wall consisted of fine twined linen hangings, suspended from sixty pillars placed at a distance of two and a half yards from each other; twenty standing on the south, twenty on the north, ten on the west, and ten on the east, from whose four central pillars hung the hanging for the gate of the court: of blue, purple, and scarlet, and fine twined linen. The material of the pillars is not mentioned; most probably it was acacia wood, and wholly or partly overlaid with brass. The sockets, the bases of the pillars were of brass. Their capitals were overlaid with silver, also the rods or crossbeams extending from pillar to pillar all the way around. Near the top of every pillar were two silver hooks to which the ends of two cords were attached, the other ends being attached to brass pins, which were fixed in the ground to keep the pillars steady and erect.

Looking at those sixty pillars, resting in sockets of brass standing as sentinels guarding the tabernacle, capped with silver, and joined together by silver rods; and the dazzling white curtains, three facts are suggested for our meditation:

1. The curtains are of fine twined linen.
2. The pillars rest in brass sockets.
3. The rods, hooks and capitals are of silver.

I. *The hangings for the court shall be of fine twined linen* (Exod. 27: 9). What is the message, O curtain, which you have for our age? If the curtain should answer it would say: "My whiteness and purity is only a faint type of the spotless purity and holiness of the saviour." If there had been only one spot on His stainless robe; if He had stumbled only in one temptation, He could never have been my Redeemer to redeem me from the burden of my sins. Only a lamb without blemish could be offered as sacrifice on the Passover.

There are teachers that teach sinless perfection. Our Lord Jesus is the only human being that ever lived on this earth without sin.

In Cambridge is a statue of Lord Byron, the great poet. If you look at the statue from a certain angle you see his noble face, the high forehead of a deep thinker with his rare imagination. If you look at it from a different point, you see a man mentally afflicted, incapable of noble thought, a declared enemy of the holy God. If a great artist would express your personality in marble, would your friends say: "What a pity that along with so much goodness there was so much sinfulness"?

Nobody would say this of our Lord. From whatever side you contemplate His deeds or words, no one would be able to detect a fault in His character. He is the only one who could say to His foes: "Which of you convinceth me of sin?" (John 8: 46). He only could respond to our need. "For such an high priest became us, who is holy, harmless, undefiled, separate from sinners, and made higher than the heavens" (Heb. 7: 26).

Pilate, you were His judge; of what crime did you convict Him? And ashamed the answer comes: "I find no fault in him."

Judas, you betrayed Him; was the fair white linen tarnished? In despair the traitor answers: "*I have sinned in that I have betrayed the innocent blood*" (Matt. 27: 4).

Centurion, you could watch Him in the darkest hour of suffering; you were there when others turned their faces from Him; did He utter bitter recriminations against His enemies, His murderers? You witnessed His last moments; people say: "People do not wear a mask in their last moments." Centurion, what is your judgment on the crucified One? And he spoke: "*Truly this was the Son of God*" (Matt. 27: 54).

Peter, you once were His disciple; you lived with Him for three years. It is said: "You only get to know a person when you live with him." You have seen Him weary after a long day's work, longing for rest. It was impossible for Him to be hidden. People thronged to bring Him their sick. Peter, have you ever seen Him impatient? He was misunderstood by His nearest kin, disappointed in His chosen disciples. Peter, you denied Him thrice. Tell us, did you observe spots on the fine linen? The hand of the old man is slightly trembling when he is writing to the strangers scattered through Pontus and Galatia. Would you like to know why he lays down his pen, why there is a tear in his eyes? Read what he has just written: "Who *did no sin,* neither was *guile* found in his mouth: who, when he was reviled, *reviled not again*; when he suffered, *he threatened not*, but committed himself to him that judgeth righteously: who his own self bare *our sins* in his *own body on the tree*, that we, being dead to sins, should live unto righteousness: by whose stripes ye were healed" (1 Pet. 2: 22–4).

Through whose stripes *I am healed*. Reader, I want you to look thoughtfully at that fine white linen. I want you to kneel at the foot of that rugged cross. Look at your Saviour dying for you on that cross. Remember, there is life in a look at the crucified one; and as you look up at Him, the holy Son of God, who died in your stead, softly repeat the words of that simple children's hymn:

> There was no other good enough
> To pay the price of sin;
> He only could unlock the gate
> Of heaven and let us in.

The tabernacle, its vessels, its court, is not only a type of Christ, but should also be a type of Christ's followers—as the head, so the members. As He walked, so ought we to walk.

The natural man has no white garment. We have all sinned and come short of the glory of God. "We are all as an unclean thing, and all *our righteousnesses* are as *filthy rags*" (Isa. 64: 6). Is it possible for me to become fine twined linen? Thanks be to God, it is. The righteousness of God, the white garment, comes "by *faith of Jesus Christ* unto all and *upon all them that believe*: for there is no difference" (Rom. 3: 22). We began this chapter with the old question: "What must I do to be saved?" The answer is: "Believe on the Lord Jesus Christ." Accept His finished work for you. He died for you; He is our righteousness. "This is his name whereby he shall be called, The Lord our Righteousness" (Jer. 23: 6).

"Now Joshua was clothed with filthy garments, and stood before the angel. And he answered and spake unto those that stood before him, saying, Take away the filthy garments from him. And unto him he said, Behold, I have caused thine iniquity to pass from thee, and I will clothe thee with change of garments" (Zech. 3: 3, 4).

Garments are habits. Repeated actions become habits. Habits grow into character. The Lord can change your character. He has done it for thousands; He can do it for you. By looking unto Jesus, your character gets changed (2 Cor. 3: 18); and He not only gives you the white garment, but He is able to keep it clean for you (Jude, verse 24).

He that hath the seven spirits of God, and the seven stars, promised the overcomers in Sardis that they shall be clothed in white raiment (Rev. 3: 5). The bride shall "be arrayed in fine linen, clean and white: for *the fine linen is the righteousness of saints*" (Rev. 19: 8). The righteousness of the saints rests on God's righteousness.

II. *The sixty pillars of the court were resting in sockets of brass.* The altar of burnt-offering was overlaid with brass; it was called *the brazen altar.* Before the priests could enter the sanctuary their hands and feet had to be cleansed in *the laver of brass.* Brass was the characteristic metal used outside the tabernacle, gold inside. In a study of the different passages in the Old Testament in which the word copper is used, we see that its symbolic meaning is strength and power: applied to God it declares His unchanging character, the impossibility to escape His *righteous judgment*, the security of being under His protection.

Brass is the symbol of God's Righteousness and Power. "As sin hath reigned unto death, even so might *grace reign through righteousness* unto eternal life by Jesus Christ our Lord" (Rom. 5: 21). Grace is on the throne, but its foundation is the righteousness of God.

"Rest on God's grace and mercy only," said a minister to his dying elder. In broken words the answer came, "I have a surer resting place still—Father's eternal justice and righteousness."

III. *The rods, the hooks and capitals of the pillars were of silver.* This silver was part of the redemption money: the half-shekel which every Israelite of twenty years and beyond, as a *ransom for his soul,* had to offer in the sanctuary. He could not join the host of Israel without having paid the ransom money; neither can we be Christ's soldiers, if we have not been redeemed by Jesus Christ. Saint Peter says: "Ye know that ye were not redeemed with corruptible things, as silver and gold . . . but with the precious blood of Christ, as of a lamb without blemish and without spot" (1 Pet. 1: 18, 19).

I am well aware that modern theology looks down despisingly on what they call "blood theology," but the Bible teaches that redemption through the precious blood of Christ is the only way for a sinner to become reconciled with God. Like a red current it runs all the way through the Bible. God promised it in Paradise to fallen man, it spoke through Abel's sacrifice, from Noah's altar, in the lamb that God provided instead of Isaac, in the Passover lamb and God's promise that the angel of death would pass the house where there was blood on the lintel and side-posts. We follow that red current in the story of Rahab, in the sacrifices on the brazen altar in Psalms and Prophets. Isaiah points to that lamb that was brought to the slaughter, that was wounded for our transgressions and bruised for our iniquities (Isa. 53: 5, 7).

We open the New Testament and Christ's forerunner, John the Baptist, pointing his disciples to the Lord, says: "Behold the lamb of God, which taketh away the sin of the world." Study the teaching of the apostles. They had only one theme: "Jesus Christ, who died for our sins and rose again for our justification." I have been a minister of the gospel now for fifty years. I was crossing the ocean in a big liner and had preached in the morning. As we were going down for dinner a steward called and asked me to go to the hospital as a sick man wanted to see me. In a few words he told me his story. He had lost his wife six months ago; he had an inward complaint and felt it was fatal. He made up his mind to say good-bye to a married daughter in New York. Up until Friday he had done all his duties. On Saturday he went to the surgeon and was examined. It was too late for an operation. He knew he was going to die. I ask you, could you suggest any other message of comfort than the one I could bring that dying man? I told him of the Saviour who loved him more than any friend, who had borne the punishment of his sins in his stead; that he had nothing to do but accept the pardon, and that the same Saviour was waiting for him and had prepared a home for him. In simple faith he put his trust in the Saviour. He asked me to give him Holy Communion, and an hour after he went peacefully home to his Saviour. I know no other comfort for a dying soul.

2

A PILLAR IN THE TEMPLE OF MY GOD

17. And *the pillars round about* the court shall be
filleted with *silver*; their hooks shall be of silver,
and ther sockets of brass.—EXODUS 27: 17

A WORD for ministers and church members.

As we have seen already, the curtains of the court of
fine twined linen were suspended by silver hooks to
the sixty pillars, of which twenty were for the north
and south side, and ten for the east and west side.

In his letter to Timothy, the apostle says that the
house of God, the church of the living God, is *the
pillar and ground of the truth.* Our blessed Lord said:
"I am the truth." The calling of the church is to manifest that truth to the world. Woe, when the church or
its members should become unfaithful to its trust. "If
the light that is in thee be darkness, how great is that
darkness!" (Matt. 6: 23).

The world does not realize what it owes to God's
children. If there had been ten righteous in Sodom and
Gomorrah, the Lord would have spared those cities for
their sake. God made Potiphar's house to prosper because of Joseph and made him a blessing to Egypt.
The little captive girl brought again sunshine in the
home of Naaman. How often unconverted children only
realize the value of praying parents when the Lord has
taken them away.

Every living member of the Church should be a pillar where the Lord has placed him. A pillar helps to support the building. Our Lord is not only our sin-bearer, but He longs to become also our burden-bearer. "Casting all your cares upon him, for he careth for you. But if you are His follower, He expects you also to become a burden-bearer. "Bear ye one another's burdens, and so fulfil the law of Christ" (Gal. 6: 2).

Will you pardon me if I ask you if you are a pillar? James, John and Peter were (Gal. 2: 9). Are you a burden-bearer in your church? Can others come to you with their troubles and be sure of a sympathetic hearing? I am quite sure Joses of Cyprus was a burden-bearer. The apostles gave him a new name; they called him Barnabas, the man who knew how to comfort others.

Forgive me, are you a burden or a burden-bearer in your family, in the office, or factory? You say you are not gifted, you are shy, you have only one talent. I think that is the case with the majority of us. There are few talented people and, therefore, most work is done by the one-talent folks. You know the Lord loves you; that is part of your talent. Use it by showing love to somebody else. The world is hungry for love. The Lord has given you His peace; that is part of your talent. Become a peace-maker. Pour oil on the troubled waters. The Lord has given you the joy of the Holy Ghost—part of your talent. Give a smile. It makes people happy. Give a smile and a handshake to a stranger; you will become a pillar in your church.

Are you a minister? I do not mean a prime-minister, but a minister in your church. A minister is a servant, a footwasher. I must confess I love the designation, Pastor. A pastor is a shepherd. Our Lord was the real Shepherd; we are under-shepherds. Paul was not only the greatest missionary, but he had the heart of a pastor. How he prayed for his converts; how great was his longing that Christ should be formed in them!

Paul was a burden-bearer—the burden of all the churches was upon him. What a compassionate heart he had—the weak members of the body were his special concern. At no price was he a stumbling-block in their path. What are you doing with the weakness, with the failures of others? Do you bring them to the sanctuary or into the camp to add other sins to them? May the Lord give you a priestly heart to leave the failures and sins of others in the sanctuary and not to spread them abroad.

A class-leader told Wesley that God had given him one special talent: he had sharp eyes to detect the failures of his members. Wesley was silent a moment and then said, "Brother, I do not think the Lord would mind your burying that talent." A burden or burden-bearer—which are you? Are you a pillar in the house of God? Of course I cannot tell whether you are a pillar or not. God knows; you know. In order to become a pillar you will have to become an overcomer and have victory in your daily life. "Him that overcometh *will I make a pillar* in the temple of my God, and he shall no more go out" (Rev. 3: 12).

We do not know for certain out of what material the pillars were made; we only know that the sockets were of brass and that their capitals were of silver. Some commentators hold that they were of acacia wood, others that they were at least partly overlaid with silver. To me this seems to be immaterial, for our God can make something out of poor material. Jacob was certainly poor material to make a saint out of, but in God's school he became an Israel. The firmness and strength of the pillars lies not in themselves but in the brass sockets. If you long to become a pillar you have to learn: I am good for nothing. "Apart from me ye can do nothing" (John 15: 5), and the second lesson: "I can do all things through Christ which strengtheneth me" (Phil. 4: 13).

Why do pillars need brass sockets? Because in their own strength they could not bear the curtains of fine twined linen. "Go ye into all the world and preach the gospel to every creature." But, Lord, do you not expect too much from us? How can we carry out such a tremendous undertaking? We poor fishermen, who never left our native country? "All power is given unto me . . . Go ye." Wherever you go I will go with you; "all power is given unto me."

Does your church present more difficulties than any other? Pillar of acacia wood, do not forget your brass socket. Be strong, but not in your own strength. "Be strong *in the Lord* and in the power of *his* might" (Eph. 6: 10).

May I be allowed to make a very obvious remark? The capital of the pillar must be overlaid with silver. How can you show others the way of salvation if you have not entered the narrow gate yourself?—poor pillar that has no brass socket; poor church that has an unconverted pastor! "I believe, and therefore have I spoken" (2 Cor. 4: 13). "Ye shall be my witnesses."

That is all the Lord requires of us. A witness can only give testimony of what he has seen and heard, what he has personally experienced. Paul said: "I am not ashamed of the gospel of Christ, for it is the power of God" (Rom. 1: 16). He had experienced that power in his own heart before he witnessed to others, and, therefore, there was power in his preaching.

When the capital is covered with silver, when the foundation is a socket of brass, when the heart is burning in love for Jesus and souls, when he have been endued with power from on high, the inevitable result is: *"We cannot but speak the things we have seen and heard"* (Acts 4: 20).

The Tabernacle and Its Court

3

THE GATE OF THE COURT

18. And the hanging for the gate of the court was needlework, of blue, and purple, and scarlet, and fine twined linen.—Exodus 38: 18

WHEN we begin the study of the tabernacle in Exodus 25, we notice that the Holy Spirit does not start with the Gate of the Court, but leads us into the Holy of Holies, where the ark and the mercy seat were and from there into the Holy Place with the table of shewbread, the candlestick, and the altar of incense, to the Court with the laver and altar of burnt-offering, to the Gate of the Court.

Salvation does not start with man, but with God. Throughout the Bible the emphasis is on God, not on man in the way of salvation. "He brought me up out of the horrible pit and miry clay" (Ps. 40: 2). The starting point is the loving heart of our Heavenly Father. Not that we loved Him first, but He loved us and loves with an everlasting love. "*God-seekers*" is a word often used in modern sermons. The Bible says: "The Lord looked down from heaven upon the children of men, to see if there were any that did understand, and seek God. They are all gone aside, they are all together become filthy: there is none that doeth good, no, not one" (Ps. 14: 2, 3). *We do not seek God;* it *is God* with His great father-heart, who with infinite love and patience is seeking the soul of man. Our blessed Lord left His heavenly home to come down on this earth to *seek and save* that which was lost.

> Oh, the love that sought me,
> Oh, the blood that bought me,
> Wondrous grace that brought me
> to the fold.

We have been thinking of the white hangings of the court suspended from sixty pillars fixed in sockets of brass and capped with silver. Did they bar the way into the sanctuary? The heavenly architect provided a gate thirty feet in length and seven and a half feet in the height and breadth. The curtain which was suspended from four pillars was of blue, purple, scarlet and fine linen.

Those who study numbers in Scripture will point out to us the prominence of the number four in the dimensions of the gate, the length being four times the width and the height, the four colours of the curtains, the life of Christ given us in the four gospels; and that four is in Scripture a symbol of life as five is of grace, seven of perfection, and three of resurrection.

Without going deeper into this interesting study, we shall all agree that the gate of the court is a beautiful symbol of Him who is the resurrection and the life, and who has said: *"I am the door: by me if any man enter in, he shall be saved"* (John 10: 9).

Blue, purple, scarlet and white were the four colours used in the embroidery of the beautiful gate—all four pointing to the Saviour.

Blue is the colour of heaven. Our Lord's home was heaven. He told Nicodemus that the Son of man came down from heaven; a heavenly host sang at His birth. He was the bread that came down from heaven; and when we read the gospels, we see how often His thoughts were in His heavenly home. Christ lived heaven on earth. People have asked me what heaven is like, what God is like. I can only answer: If you want to know what God is like, read the gospels; study the Lord Jesus Christ in His words and deeds, and you will know what God is. Christ says: "He that has seen me has seen the Father."

Paul says our conversation is in heaven. We lead a heavenly life on earth. Can you say that? The Israelites had to wear a *ribband of blue* on the fringe of their garments (Num. 15: 38). It showed them as heavenly, doing God's will on earth as it is done in heaven. Do your family and your companions notice your blue ribband?

Purple is a sign of His royalty, of His majesty. When Pilate asked the Lord: "Art thou a king then?" the Lord's answer was: "Thou sayest that I am a king" (John 18: 37). When Christ came on earth, He emptied Himself of His glory. Only to a few it was given to see the purple. The *blind* beggar in Jericho had seen the purple when he cried for help to the Son of David. The Canaanite woman did; with her great faith she saw in Him her royal master. St. John did: "We beheld his glory, the glory as of the only begotten of the Father, full of grace and truth" (John 1: 14).

The day will come, it may be soon, "that at the name of Jesus every knee should bow . . . and that every tongue should confess that Jesus Christ is Lord, to the glory of God the Father" (Phil. 2: 10, 11). How often have you prayed "Thy kingdom come"? Have you made obeisance to the man in purple? Have you acknowledged Christ as your absolute King? Mary felt for the man in purple when she said, "Rabboni," my master.

Scarlet is the translation of two Hebrew words. In Psalm 22: 6 "to laath" has been translated worm, "*I am a worm*, and no man; a reproach of men, and despised of the people." The other word "shahl" is found in Isaiah 1: 18, "Though your *sins be as scarlet*, they shall be as white as snow."

Scarlet, a deep red, points to the sufferings of our Saviour. "He was clothed with a vesture dipped in blood: and his name is called The Word of God" (Rev. 19: 13).

The fine white linen shows the stainless purity of His human character. "Who did no sin, neither was guile found in his mouth: who, when he was reviled, reviled not again; when he suffered, he threatened not; but committed himself to him that judgeth righteously" (1 Pet. 2: 22, 23). Blue, purple, scarlet and white, the four colours of the gate of the court, a symbol of our Lord. He is the man from heaven, the King of kings, the man of sorrows and acquainted with grief, the Son of man, the Son of God, the man Christ Jesus. "In him," says John, "was life; and the life was the light of men" (John 1: 4).

In the four gospels, Matthew shows Him as the King foretold by the prophets; Mark, as the Servant of Jehovah going about doing good; Luke, as the Son of man seeking the lost; John, as the Son of God, the only begotten of the Father.

I close this chapter with some lines from my Bible: May my last thought in the evening, my first thought in the morning, be of:

A dying Saviour's love,
A risen Saviour's power,
An ascended Saviour's grace,
A coming Saviour's glory.

4

SALVATION ONLY IN CHRIST

11. This is the stone which was set at nought of
you builders, which is become the head of the corner.
12. Neither is there salvation in any other: for
there is none other name under heaven given among
men, whereby we must be saved.—ACTS 4: 11, 12

THE gate of the court, the outer vail of the tabernacle, the inner vail before the Holy of holies, were
all three in a straight line. All three had the same
colours in their embroidery: blue, purple, scarlet and
white; and all three are types of the same Saviour. You
need Him, to enter the court as a lost sinner, to seek
God's forgiveness through the blood of Christ; you need
him when you enter the sanctuary to serve your Lord;
you need him in order to have fellowship with your
Father which seeth in secret. Whether in the court or
in the Holy Place, or in the Holiest of all, you are
accepted "in the beloved."

There is *only one gate* to the court, one door to the
tabernacle, one vail to the Holiest of all. There is only
one way for a sinner to become reconciled with God.
Jesus said: "I am the way, the truth, and the life: no
man cometh unto the Father, but by me" (John 14: 6).
It is true we may reach the court in very different ways.
The Holy Spirit does not treat us all alike after one
pattern; neither does He want to make us all alike.

34

Some fortunate ones are in early childhood led by mother's hand to the gate of the court; they hardly remember the time that they were not in the court. Others wandered away into a far country and it was a thorny path that led them to the gate. The change was so great that they can easily tell you the day and hour when they went through the gate of the court. It is not important when and how you arrived at the gate, but that you have passed through it at all. It needed an earthquake for the jailer to open his heart to the Lord. The Holy Spirit opened Lydia's heart as a tender rosebud unfolds its petals.

Only one way. Jesus is the way. Many have in vain tried to slip under the curtains. "Not by works of righteousness which we have done, but *according to his mercy he saved us,* by the washing of regeneration, and renewing of the Holy Ghost" (Titus 3: 5).

People still ask with the young ruler: *"What must I do* to be saved?" The answer is, "Believe on the Lord Jesus." Trust His finished work and thou shalt be saved. Dr. Torrey, as an experienced soul-winner, answered a man who told him that however hard he tried he could not find peace, "Friend, there is only a difference of two letters between your religion and mine, but they make all the difference in the world. You belong to the 'do religion'; I belong to the 'done religion.'"

Jesus said, "It is finished." Jesus is the way, not the church. Your baptism will not bring you to heaven, neither will the Lord's supper, however highly I esteem these means of grace. You may be a church member, a faithful attendant at church. But the church cannot save you. It is not sufficient that you can give me a clear description of the gate. You may have clear, Scriptural ideas about the way of salvation, or if you wish, of the way of sanctification. Your knowledge will not save you; on the contrary, it will make your condemnation all the more severe if you do not act up to it. If I am saved, it is not my knowledge that has saved me, but a person, and that person is our Lord Jesus.

You yourself must enter the gate; nobody can enter for you in your stead. Jesus can "save to the uttermost all *that come* unto God by him" (Heb. 7: 25), but you must come. Your good father, your saintly mother, your beloved child cannot enter the gate for you. Salvation is a personal matter; you cannot be saved by proxy. Jesus said: "I am the living bread which came down from heaven: if any man *eat of this bread,* he shall live for ever" (John 6: 51). "If any man thirst, let him *come unto me,* and drink" (John 7: 37). No one can eat or drink for you; you must do this yourself. The Lord bids you come to Him; He invites you to come; you must accept the invitation.

I pray that the Lord may use these meditations for the edifying of God's people, but also for the salvation of precious souls. Will you pause a moment? Just lay down the book; ask yourself the question: Have I come? Have I entered the gate? Am I saved? Have I accepted the invitation?

Christ has suffered in your stead; He has borne your sins on His cross. He has won you your pardon. You must accept it, otherwise the atonement will not avail you. Dr. Richardson tells us of a prisoner sentenced to death. Many people had interceded for him. Only a few days before the execution a messenger from the

Home Office arrived with the pardon. The governor went into the death cell and told the prisoner that a reprieve had come. The man said he had finished with life; he did not want a pardon. The governor informed the Home Secretary and asked if they were to carry on with the preparations for the execution. The answer came: "A pardon that is not accepted is only a scrap of paper."

Jesus is the door and *the door is still open*. A widow was living on a small pension with her daughter in the country. She had never told her child the misery of her married life; that her husband, a teacher, had died of drink. The child grew up, a fine girl carefully trained by a loving mother; she had never tasted a drop of drink. At a birthday party she was offered a glass of wine. She refused; they teased her. At last she took the glass and swallowed it in a gulp. She became a secret drinker. One day she disappeared and in vain the mother tried to trace her. Rumours reached the village that she was seen on the streets of the city. The mother kept praying for her erring child. It was certainly the Holy Spirit who suggested to her to have her picture printed. Beneath it she wrote herself: "Mother loves you still, come home." One evening the girl entered a refuge home of the Salvation Army. A group of girls stood around the picture. The girl came nearer and recognized her mother's face, her mother's writing. With a loud cry she fell on the floor. The little Salvation Army captain (God bless the Salvation Army) had her laid on her bed. When the others were gone and all was quiet, she took the girl to her heart. The girl sobbed out her story, and the good woman told her of her Saviour's love, who loved her even more than her mother, and who would help her to become again her mother's sunshine. Did she believe what mother said? Would she go back to mother?

I do not know what she wrote to mother, what the good captain wrote, but the angels read it and rejoiced over it. The girl had gone through the gate of the court. Have you?

Some days afterwards, late in the evening, the people of the village had all gone to bed. Only in mother's cottage still burned a light. Softly she tried the door— it was not locked. There stood mother with open arms. I do not know what they spoke; the Lord knows. Upstairs was her little room, the little bed, the white sheets and curtains, forget-me-nots on the table. Mother put the tired child to bed, prayed with her, smiled at her, blessed her. And as the girl, resting on mother's shoulder, asked, "Mother, do you not lock the door at night?" the mother answered, "Darling, ever since you left, the door has been open. I have always been waiting for you to come home." An open door, a waiting Saviour.

Have you come home? Will you not come home now? The door is open. Jesus says: *"Come unto me, all ye that labour and are heavy laden, and I will give you rest"* (Matt. 11: 28). *"Him that cometh to me I will in no wise cast out"* (John 6: 37).

5

THE BRAZEN ALTAR, A TYPE OF OUR LORD

> 1. And thou shalt make an altar of *acacia* wood, five cubits long, and five cubits broad; the altar shall be *foursquare*: and the height thereof shall be three cubits.
>
> 2. And thou shalt make *the horns* of it upon the four corners thereof: his horns shall be of the same: and thou shalt *overlay it with brass.*
>
> 6. And thou shalt make staves for the altar, staves of *acacia wood,* and overlay them with *brass.*
>
> 8. *Hollow* with boards shalt thou make it: *as* it was shewed thee in the mount, *so* shall they make it.
>
> —Exodus 27: 1, 2, 6, 8

WE have entered the gate of the court. The desert is behind us. We stand within the holy precincts. The question naturally arises: Why did God command this holy place, His dwelling place amidst the people, to be in three separate divisions: the court, the sanctuary, and the Holiest of all?

Five hundred years the children of Israel had dwelt in Egypt, strangers in a strange land. Their numbers had greatly increased. A king ascended the throne, who did not know Joseph and did not know how much Egypt owed those strangers. He feared their numbers. They might ally themselves to his enemies and dispossess him as he had done his predecessor. He determined to exterminate those undesirable aliens. He did not succeed. No one will—Israel is God's covenanted people.

The Brazen Altar

A wonderful future is still awaiting them. God led them out of the house of bondage with His mighty arm.

They were now in the desert on the way to Canaan. The Lord wanted to reveal Himself to His people. This revelation necessarily had to be progressive. They were like little children. Israel had not passed unscathed through Egypt; they had much to learn and to unlearn. They were in the kindergarten stage. They did not learn quickly, but the teacher was patient. He gave them object-lessons and taught them through pictures. The tabernacle with its furniture, and the different sacrifices were a wonderful object-lesson. They showed them sin and its dire consequences, but also a way of reconciliation between a holy God and His sinful people. Jesus Christ is the way; and the tabernacle, its court, sanctuary, and Holy place, its furniture and offerings, should show the Israelites the way of salvation and point to Christ, the wisdom of God who has been made unto us *wisdom* and *righteousness* and *sanctification* and *redemption* (1 Cor. 1: 30).

The court is the place where the prodigal finds his way back to Father's house, where lost sinners become obedient and cleansed children of God. In the court we are covered with the precious blood of Christ, the lamb without spot. The court is the first grade in Father's school. With grateful hearts the little ones learn to spell the word *reconciliation*. No one can come to God who has not passed through the court. Our Lord is the living way to Father's heart. The Lord God sent Adam forth out of Eden and placed at the East of the garden Cherubims with a flaming sword. The sword of divine justice pierced our Saviour's heart and through His heart goes the living way to the heart of our Father in heaven.

The sanctuary could be entered only by priests. Our Lord has made us "kings and priests unto God and His Father" (Rev. 1: 6). "We are an holy priesthood to offer up spiritual sacrifices, acceptable to God by Jesus Christ" (1 Pet. 2: 5). The Bible teaches the universal priesthood of all believers—saved to serve. "That he would grant unto us, that we being delivered out of the hand of our enemies might serve him without fear" (Luke 1: 74). Only those who at the brazen altar have been delivered from the burden of their sins and have been cleansed at the laver can render God acceptable service. One of the reasons why God in such a remarkable way blessed Dr. R. A. Torrey's missionary tour around the world was that he always insisted on new converts starting at once to win others for Christ—saved to serve. The *Holy of holies* could only be entered once a year by the high priest on the day of atonement, and that not without blood. When Christ died for us, *the veil of the temple* was rent in twain. It was a type of the human body of Christ. Now a new and living way is opened and *all* God's children may have free access and uninterrupted communion with their Father in heaven (Heb. 10: 20).

The brazen altar would at once draw the attention of a worshipper when he entered the gate. It was called the brazen altar to distinguish it from the golden altar of incense in the Holy Place. Copper was the metal mostly used in the court, gold in the inner sanctuary. It was also called the *table of the Lord* (Mal. 1: 12).

The burnt-offering which the Levites offered on it was called *the bread of the Lord* (Lev. 21: 6). Every offering had first to be brought to the altar of burnt-offering. It was of greater dimensions than any other furniture of the tabernacle; it was the centre of the worship. To show its pre-eminence, we find that in Exodus 29: 44 it was simply called *the altar.*

Let us make a mental picture of the altar. I have already mentioned that it was larger than any other vessel in the tabernacle; they could indeed all find room in it. The altar was made of acacia wood. This might at first surprise us, as a constant fire had to be maintained in it. We, therefore, read that it was overlaid with brass or copper—acacia wood overlaid with copper. It was foursquare, nine feet in length and nine feet in breadth. It was five feet high. Around the altar at the top was a compass, a border or rim similar to the crown of gold around the altar of incense. There was a grate of network brass. Commentators have differed in placing this grate. I take it to be the lower part of the altar, going halfway up with a ledge which served as a shelf for the priest to stand on when he was arranging the sacrifice—two and a half feet from the ground, easily reached by a gentle slope of earth. We notice that at each of the four corners was a horn made of acacia wood overlaid with brass, and that there were staves for the altar made of acacia wood covered with brass, going through four brazen rings attached to the four corners. We also notice that the ashpans, shovels, basins, fleshhooks, and firepans were all made of brass.

Finally we shall not forget that the altar was hollow, without floor resting on the earth, and made of different plates joined together. *As* it was shown to Moses on the mount, *so* it had to be made.

As we are able now to have a clear conception of the altar and have noticed the important points, let us pray that the Holy Spirit may help us to see the significance of each point, always bearing in mind that the altar is a type given us by God of His blessed Son. Paul's greatest longing was to know Christ; he was ready to surrender all for the excellency of the knowledge of Christ.

The altar had to be made of acacia wood and overlaid with brass—not the wood without the brass; not the brass without the wood.

The shittim tree or acacia tree grew in the desert. The bush Moses saw in the wilderness might well have been a wild acacia tree. Its wood was white and durable. Higher critics might express it unlikely that an altar on which the fire should not go out should be made of wood. God said: "Thou shalt make an altar of acacia wood."

Acacia wood is a symbol of Christ's humanity, His human nature; the brass with which it was overlaid, the righteous divine judgment of sin. Need I point out that Christ had a divine hatred of sin? How His sensitive nature must have suffered as He saw the havoc sin had wrought in men! He knew the thoughts of men and had no need to be told. He saw the evil that proceeded out of a corrupt heart. He knew that the Holy God could not let sin go by unpunished.

Christ is perfect man and perfect God. Well might we ask with the virgin: "How shall this thing be?" We cannot explain the incarnation. It is a mystery God manifested in the flesh. From the earliest ages the

Church has taught us in her creeds, "Who for us men and for our salvation came down from heaven, and was incarnate by the Holy Ghost of the Virgin Mary and was made man." It is one of the main pillars of our faith. "The soul that sinneth it shall die." Either the lamb at the passover had to die or the firstborn. If Christ had to bear our sins, He had to die for us. And not only had He to take upon Himself our human nature, but that human nature had to be spotless and undefiled, a lamb without spot or blemish. Who knew no sin, God made sin for us (2 Cor. 5 : 21).

The incarnation is a pillar of our faith. Not that in the incarnation Christ took fallen man into union with Himself; the incarnation without Christ's death and resurrection could not have reconciled us with God, but His divine nature gave that sacrifice its infinite value; a full, sufficient sacrifice and oblation for the sins of the whole world.

Our heavenly Father in His infinite love had foreseen the fall of the human race, and even before the foundation of the world had provided the means of reconciliation. In paradise He pointed out to our fallen parents that evil should not be victorious, that the *woman's seed* should bruise Satan's head. Need I point out that this expression, "woman's seed," occurs only once in the Bible and points out the wonderful birth of the Redeemer? Does it not find its explanation in the word God spake through the prophet Isaiah: "Behold, a *virgin* shall conceive, and bear a son, and shall call his name Immanuel" (Isa. 7 : 14).

God so loved the world and you, that He sent His Son; but listen, that Son was willing to come, and loved you enough to die for you. How I pray that the Holy Spirit may use this chapter to make Christ precious to you! Christ was not a martyr. No Roman governor could have forced Him on that cross. He was a willing victim. He said: "Therefore doth my Father love me, because I *lay down my life*, that I might take it again. *No man taketh it from me*, but I lay it down of myself" (John 10: 17, 18). Brazen altar, thou art a symbol of Christ and His infinite love for fallen men, His supreme sacrifice. Thou art to me, also, a symbol of His rugged cross. May I often in quiet meditation kneel at its foot, and may it be my heart's prayer:

> Lord Jesus, make Thyself to me
> A living bright reality,
> More vivid to faith's vision keen
> Than anything on earth can be.

"Thou shalt overlay it with brass"—a brazen altar. Brass everywhere in the court: a symbol of *divine justice*—not human justice that may err, that may be influenced by outward circumstances, and has not always had its eyes bandaged. Divine justice does not err: "The Lord will not hold him guiltless that taketh his name in vain" (Exod. 20: 7). It is a divine decree: "The soul that sinneth, it shall die" (Ezek. 18: 4). "The wages of sin is death" (Rom. 6: 23). God sent His Son. Do you realize what that meant for God the Father? Do you think if there had been any other way for the human race to be reconciled with God, would He not have chosen it? The altar was overlaid with brass—divine justice. Christ was the Altar, divine justice personified. His greatest wish was to do Father's will, to see Father

glorified. Listen to what Christ says: "The Lord God hath opened mine ear, and I was not rebellious, neither turned away back. *I gave my back to the smiters*, and my cheeks to them that plucked off the hair: *I hid not my face from shame and spitting*" (Isa. 50: 5, 6). Read those words again and again, and tell me would Christ have chosen that way if there had been any other possibility to satisfy the eternal principles of divine justice, and to lift up to Father's heart His fallen children? No, friends, there was no other way. Christ took our place. "The Lord hath laid on him the iniquity of us all. He was wounded for *my transgressions*, he was bruised for *my iniquities*: the chastisement of *my peace* was upon him, and with his stripes *I am* healed" (Isa. 53: 5, 6). Only an altar of acacia, overlaid with brass: only a man partaking of flesh and blood, a perfect man, a sinless man, could suffer in our stead and die; only a man could be the last Adam. "There is one God, and one mediator between God and men, *the man Christ Jesus*" (2 Tim. 2: 5).

6

THE ALTAR OF BURNT-OFFERING
AND THE SIN-OFFERING

4. He shall bring the bullock unto the door of the
tabernacle of the congregation *before the Lord*; and
shall lay his hand upon the bullock's head, and the
priest *shall kill* the bullock before the Lord.

12. Even the whole bullock shall he carry forth
without the camp unto a clean place, where the ashes
are poured out, and *burn him on the wood with fire*:
where the ashes are poured out shall he be burnt.

—LEVITICUS 4: 4, 12

THE Altar of Burnt-offering is a type of our blessed
Lord. It is also a symbol of the cross. Christ was
the altar, but also the lamb that was slain on the
altar.

Let us approach once more in holy reverence. It was
foursquare. He was the only perfect man that ever
lived. Study the balance in His character, His humility,
His majesty, washing His disciples' feet, the servant of
all; meeting majestically the band who had come to take
Him. "Whom seek ye?" Awestruck, they fell to the
ground. Burning with indignation at the hypocrisy of
Pharisee and Sadducee, He tenderly dismissed a woman
taken in adultery. Read the Gospels; follow the Lord
as He went through the land. Did you ever find Him
in a hurry, or unwilling when interrupted? He had put
His times in Father's hand (Ps. 31: 5) and, therefore

could abide Father's hour, always living in harmony with Father's will.

The altar had four sides and each side tells us of a special gracious gift we receive out of His hands:

1. *The forgiveness of sins.* This is the good news which one side of the altar brings us. However stained with sin a soul may be, the blood shed can cleanse him. "Come now, and let us reason together, saith the Lord: though your sins be as scarlet, they shall be as white as snow" (Isa. 1: 18).

2. *Substitution,* another side promises us. How precious for a sin-burdened soul! "All we like sheep have gone astray; . . . the Lord hath laid on him the iniquity of us all" (Isa. 53: 6). If He has taken the burden from my shoulders, I need not feel the weight any more. This teaches the second side of the altar.

3. *Reconciling the Father and the sinner through the Son* is found at the brazen altar. Our great High Priest takes the hand of the repenting sinner and with the other He touches Father's hand. "For there is one God, and one mediator between God and men, the man Christ Jesus" (1 Tim. 2: 5). He can save to the uttermost them that come through Him to God (Heb. 7: 25). That is the third side of the altar.

4. *Deliverance from the bondage of sin* you may find at the altar, when you are willing to become a burnt-offering yourself, and lay on the altar, being made comformable to His death, reckoning yourselves to be *dead unto sin,* but alive unto God through Jesus Christ our Lord (Rom. 6: 11). The cross will not only cover our sins, but it *will cover us.* If the cross covers me, it is a matter of course that it covers my sins; and we find

in the brazen altar a saving, a freeing, a keeping power. This is the fourth side of the altar.

"*And thou shalt make the horns of it upon the four corners thereof*" (Exod. 27: 2). The horns of a mighty stag are his ornament; they may serve as defence and protection. They speak to us of *might* and *strength*. "He shall give strength unto his king, and exalt the horn (the power) of his anointed" (1 Sam. 2: 10). "The horn of Moab is cut off" (his power is broken) (Jer. 48: 25). "For thou art the glory of their strength: and in thy favour our horn shall be exalted" (our power increased) (Ps. 89: 17).

These passages will suffice to show us that the four horns of the altar point out the powerful value of Christ's sacrifice; and as they point to all four directions, it seems as if they want to tell us: "Look unto me, and be ye saved, *all the ends of the earth*: for I am *God, and there is none else*" (Isa. 45: 22).

Adonijah fled for protection to the corners of the altar. He had plotted to seize the kingdom out of the hands of his aged father and to be acclaimed king instead of Solomon. Clasping the horns of the altar, he was safe from his brother's wrath. Solomon allowed him to go to his own house (1 Kings 1: 50–53). How often have I, as a student, looked at the heavy knocker of Durham's cathedral. Whatever the crime of the fugitive, when he raised that knocker, claiming the right of asylum, he was safe within the sacred precincts. "He that dwelleth in the secret place of the most High shall abide under the shadow of the Almighty" (Ps. 91: 1).

But how could the horns of the altar afford protection? Do you not see that they were sprinkled with blood? Death had already been there; the sword of justice had done its work. It was the blood, and the blood only, that gave the horns their protective power. All the sacrifices had to be brought to the altar of burnt-offering. There God met the sinner. There were two kinds of offerings: the sweet-savour offerings (the burnt-offerings), and the meal-offering (the peace-offering). These typify Christ in His perfect, sinless life, living for His Father and Father's glory. The sweet-savour offerings were prompted by the love and gratitude of the worshipper.

The non-sweet-savour offerings were the trespass-offering and the sin-offering. The trespass-offering partook in some ways of the nature of the sin-offering; it lays weight rather upon the harm done by sin than on the guilt incurred. The trespassing might be due to ignorance, but whatever harm was done to others had to be made good. As evidence of the reality of the sorrow, the harm had to be confessed, and restoration should be made. Zacchaeus proved the reality of his conversion by restoring fourfold the money which he had obtained by false accusations. I do not think many people doubted the genuineness of his conversion. It is most desirable that, when dealing with enquirers, they should be urged to seek forgiveness and make restoration wherever they have wronged others, as well as seeking forgiveness of God. This is not always an easy thing to do, and the devil may suggest many reasons not to do so, but obedience in this respect gives hope for growth and future life.

When we now meditate together on the sin-offering, we are depending especially on the teaching of the Holy

Spirit, for our subject will really be Christ and the sinner: the sinner in his need; the Saviour in His fullness and love. Christ glorified the Father, the Holy Spirit glorifies Christ; may we glorify the Holy Spirit in listening to Him, that Christ may become more precious to us than ever before.

There were three grades of sin-offerings, depending on the culprit: whether he was a priest, an official, or a private person. Sin does not only injure the sinner himself, but others in the third and fourth generation. The innocent suffer with the guilty. We all know this; we have seen it. Sin is not a weakness; sin is a hateful thing. Like a stone thrown into the water, so sin spreads in ever-widening circles. God puts the priest first. Sin in God's children is worse than sin of the unconverted. The sin of Achan caused Israel to be defeated. It may keep relatives from making a decision for the Lord. People in authority have great influence. Happy is the state whose leaders seek guidance from God. To the third group belonged the ordinary people. A bullock *without blemish* as offering for the priest; a kid of the goats, a male *without blemish* for an official; a kid of the goats, a lamb, a female without blemish for the common people.

May you and I feel our Lord present as I point out what God required in the sin-offering. The sinner himself had in each case to bring himself the offering to the altar. He had to press his hand hard, to lean upon the sin-offering. Listen, I want to speak softly. You have to slay the sin-offering. The priest shall take the blood and put it with his finger on the horns of the altar. The fat of the animal the priest shall burn on the altar. The whole animal shall be carried without the camp and burnt on the wood with fire in a clean place where the ashes are poured out.

Do you see that man with bowed head slowly passing the numerous tents of his tribe going towards the gate of the court? He is leading a little lamb without blemish; he is bringing a sin-offering. The Holy Spirit has convicted him of sin, sin against God and his fellow-men. Men did not know it. God knows. His conscience does not give him rest. Even when he lies down, his sin follows him. He arises; he chooses the lamb for an offering.

1. *He shall bring a bullock* unto the door. No servant, no friend, neither parent nor child can go for you. It matters not whether you are priest or ruler, this must be a personal transaction between you and God, a talk under four eyes with the Saviour. The woman at the well had such a talk with the Saviour. It was the first step to a life of useful service. Paul had it on the way to Damascus. He discovered that all he had been so proud of was of no value in the sight of God. His good works were nothing but splendid sins. All the credit had to be transferred to the debit side. He became spiritually bankrupt.

Reader, if you have had no Damascus hour yet in your life, will you now go to the brazen altar? Looking up into those loving, yet searching eyes of your Saviour, pray: *"Search me, O God,* and *know my heart: try me* and *know my thoughts*: and see if there be any wicked way in me, and lead me in the way everlasting" (Ps. 139: 23, 24).

2. *He shall lay his hand upon the sacrifice.* Have you done this? It is the next act. You are burdened by

your sins, do what the Lord tells you. It is so simple.
Never mind whether you have any feeling about it; do
what you are told. *Lay your hand* upon the lamb, press
hard, lean hard. When you do this, something will
happen. God will take your sins and lay them on Jesus.
he said so: *"The Lord* hath *laid on him* the *iniquity
of us all"* (Isa. 53: 6 a). Bunyan's burden rolled from his
back. Does the burden of your sin still weigh you down?
No, it is gone. How do you know? God said so. "The
priest shall make atonement for him and his sins *shall
be forgiven him.* Four times in Leviticus 4 God repeats
this statement.

There is even more. Look at the lamb! Do you see
any spot, any blemish in it? Listen, dear soul, what I
am going to tell you seems almost too good to be true.
The blamelessness of the lamb now becomes the repen-
tant sinner's blamlessness. "Blessed is the man unto
whom the Lord *imputeth* not iniquity" (Ps. 32: 2).
Blessed indeed, but God according to the riches of His
grace does far more. Abraham's faith was *imputed* to
him as righteousness. God's righteousness is Christ. He
imputes Christ to us. Does the Bible tell us what impu-
tation means? Look at that run-away slave. His punishment might be death. He is standing before his master.
Philemon has a letter in his hand, a letter from his friend,
Paul. He looks at the slave who has wronged him. The
stern look makes way to a smile. What did he read?
"Receive him as myself," reckon to him my merit. If he
has wronged you, I will repay it. That is what *imputa-
tion* means. God looks on you, on me, *in the beloved.*

3. *He shall slay the offering.* I would fain have spared
you this. It seems too terrible. No longer is it the Roman

soldiers who crucified the Lord. I slew Him. I pierced His hands and His feet. It is I that crucified Him. My sins brought Him on that cross. He paid the penalty; He bore the punishment for my sins. *He died for me.* Come with me to Golgotha. Look at your Saviour, bleeding for you on that rugged cross. Let me come close to you. I want to whisper something in your ear. Let me say it softly. It came from those parched lips: *"Greater love hath no man than this, that a man lay down his life for his friends. Ye are my friends, if ye do whatsoever I command you"* (John 15: 13, 14).

Sir Arthur Simpson, a child of God, an eminent surgeon, who in 1845 discovered the use of chloroform, writes in his autobiography: "I was a boy of twelve. When we boys came out of school I saw a sight I have never forgotten: a man was tied to a cab. His back was bare. As he was dragged through the streets the scourge fell on his back, blow after blow. His back was bleeding. What had he done? He had taken a parcel from a mail coach. It was the last time that a man was openly punished for that crime. Did anybody stop that cab and offer to take his stripes?—nobody. Jesus did for me; with His stripes I am healed. Some years afterward, coming from college, I saw another sight. A man was led out of prison. On the market was a scaffold; he was to be publicly hanged. What had he done? He had stolen a sheep. It was the last time anybody was publicly hanged. Did anybody offer to take his place?—nobody. Christ took my punishment and died for me. 'He was wounded for our transgressions, he was bruised for our iniquities: the chastisement of our peace was upon him; and with his stripes we are healed' (Isa. 53: 5)."

The fat of the animal the priest shall burn on the altar. The sin-offering was not to be sacrificed on the brazen altar. It had to be burned outside the camp, but its fat was to be offered on the altar. There was in the sin-offering, too, a sweet-smelling savour. How often I have read Isaiah 53 on Good Friday. I often halted at the tenth verse. *"It pleased the Lord to bruise him."* Need I tell you that although Christ bore the *punishment of our sin, the taint of sin never touched Him.* He was the Holy Son of God also on the cross. "The cup which my Father has given me shall I not drink it?" That loving obedience to His Father's will, the consciousness that during those dark hours of suffering He was pleasing His Father, that His Father loved Him, because of His laying down His life: this was the ray of light in the awful gloom hanging over that cross. The Father suffered with the Son, but the filial obedience of His beloved Son pleased Father's heart.

The whole bullock he shall carry forth without the camp. I cannot exhaust the meaning of this chapter. May the Holy Spirit lead you through it. I only quote Scripture. "And they took Jesus and led him away. And he bearing his cross went forth into a place called the place of a skull, which is called in Hebrew Golgotha" (John 19: 16, 17). "Wherefore Jesus also, that he might *sanctify the people with his own blood,* suffered without the gate. Let us go forth therefore unto him without the camp, bearing his reproach" (Heb. 13: 12, 13).

"That I may know him, and the power of his resurrection, and the fellowship of his sufferings, being made *conformable* unto his death" (Phil. 3: 10).

Do you see that heap of ashes?—the whole offering burnt to ashes. Christ was not conquered. He remained conqueror. His greatest victory was won when nailed to the cross. He cried with a loud voice, *"It is finished"* (John 19: 30). He suffered and was buried, and the *third day he rose again* according to the Scriptures, Christ's resurrection, the Gibraltar of our faith, the proof that Father had accepted the sin-offering on the brazen altar.

"There is therefore now *no condemnation to them which are in Christ Jesus"* (Rom. 8: 1). Christ paid the penalty, no longer the law has a hold on us. I take you to a churchyard in the country in Holland. A very simple gravestone with only four words inscribed on it: "He died for me." It was the time that Napoleon the First ruled over Holland. Constant levies were held. Napoleon needed soldiers, and a father of a large family was recruited. A friend offered to go in his stead, and he came back severely wounded and died at home. Gratitude put those words on the gravestone. Two years afterward a French officer again recruited for the war with Russia. Again the same man was taken. He replied to the military commission, "I am dead." He took the officer to the grave of his friend—"He died for me."

The new theology has no longer room for the atonement, and doubts its morality, and stutters at what they like to call "the blood theology." I can only answer, atonement is taught all through the Bible. The Holy Spirit teaches us that it is the only way for men to become reconciled with God. I believe there is far more in the atonement than the human mind can conceive. I cannot explain it. When I finish with the following illustration, I do not wish to state that it clears away all the difficulties. Of the atonement, even the greatest theologians have to say: "We know in part, and we prophesy in part. But when that which is perfect is come, then that which is in part shall be done away" (1 Cor. 13: 9, 10).

An eastern legend tells us of a young prince who had just ascended the throne. During his minority, for many years, the government had been in the hands of his mother. She was proud and loved to rule; it was not easy for her to put the reins in the hands of her son.

There was a hostile party plotting a revolution. Strange to say, some of the most important decisions of the cabinet, state secrets, leaked out and came into the hands of the enemy. When this happened a second time, the king issued an edict that whoever the guilty person might be should be openly scourged in the market place. Investigations were made, traces led to the royal palace, and it was found that the old queen was the guilty person. This became known. The people said, "The king will not have his own mother punished, there is one law for the rich and another for the poor."

A public dais was raised on the market place. The judges and nobles had taken their seats, people had come from far and near to witness the trial. At twelve o'clock the gates of the palace were opened; the king appeared and leaning heavily on his arm the trembling woman. The court opened, witnesses were heard and in profound silence the verdict was given: "Guilty." Already an officer had laid his hand on the shoulder of the guilty woman to lead her to the whipping post. Then the young king sprang from his throne, he bared his back, and blow upon blow fell upon it, till with bleeding back he was carried into the palace. Was it right? The principle of equal justice was more firmly established for the good of the kingdom than ever before. No one could say, "There is one law for the rich, another for the poor." Nor did the king ask any of his nobles to bear the punishment instead of his mother. He took it himself. *"God was in Christ, reconciling the world to himself"* (2 Cor. 5: 19). *"Mercy and truth are met together; righteousness and peace have kissed each other"* (Ps. 85: 10). "If we confess our sins, he is *faithful and just* to forgive us our sins, and to cleanse us from all unrighteousness" (1 John 1: 9).

7

THE BURNT-OFFERING AND FULL SURRENDER

> 3. If his offering be a burnt-sacrifice of the herd,
> let him offer a male *without blemish*: he shall offer it
> of his own *voluntary will* at the door of the taber-
> nacle of the congregation before the Lord.
> 4. And he shall put his hand upon the head of the
> burnt-offering; and it shall be *accepted for him to
> make atonement* for him.
> 5. And he shall kill the bullock before the Lord.
>   —LEVITICUS 1: 3, 4, 5

WE have meditated together on the sin-offering:
Christ bearing our sins on the cross, suffering in our
stead the punishment due to our sins, and reconciling
us with God. In the sin-offering the man-ward aspect
is most prominent.

The burnt-offering typifies the God-ward aspect of
Christ's life, a type of Christ in consecration. "Then
said I, Lo, *I come to do thy will.*" Christ told us that
the purpose of His coming on the earth was to do God's
will. He was the only man that ever lived on earth
who never for a single moment swerved from putting
God first in His life, to accomplish God's will. When
the disciples urged the Lord to eat, He told them that
His meat was to do the will of His Father who had
sent Him and to finish His work (John 4: 34). When
His brothers urged Him to go up to Jerusalem to the
feast, He told them His hour had not come yet. He

could abide Father's time. He could say, "I seek not mine own will, but the will of the Father which hath sent me" (John 5: 30). At the close of His life, Christ could say, "I have finished the work which thou gavest me to do" (John 17: 4). "I have glorified thee on the earth." It was a life wholly depending on His Father. "The Son can do nothing of himself, but what he seeth the Father do" (John 5: 19).

Christ was the burnt-offering. Not only when as our substitute He bore sins on the cross was He that, but also during His whole life in His whole-hearted surrender to the will of His Father, leaving us an example, that we should follow in His steps (1 Pet. 1: 21). Every fact in the life of our Saviour should become a factor in our lives. He was born that we might be born again; He died on the cross that our self-life might be crucified with Him; He rose the third day that we should rise in the newness of life with Him; He ascended into heaven that we might sit with Him in heavenly places. He became a burnt-offering that each of His followers should become a burnt-offering. "I beseech you therefore, brethren, by the mercies of God, that ye present your bodies a *living sacrifice*, holy, acceptable unto God, which is your reasonable service" (Rom. 12: 1).

Let us take our stand at the brazen altar, being conscious of the Master's presence and His words sinking deep into our hearts: "So much I did for thee, what doest thou for me?"

Your burnt-offering must be of your own free voluntary will. The Lord repeatedly emphasizes this. He will stand at the door of your heart knocking, but He will never cross the threshold unless you open Him the door. He wants no compulsory service. I once received a blank piece of paper with only the signature underneath. Some weeks before I had been speaking with the writer and urged her to a full surrender. She felt doubtful, fearing the Lord would ask something which was beyond her strength. In an accompanying letter she wrote, "I want the Lord to fill in where He wants me to go and what He wants me to do." The Lord had made her willing. Do not be afraid to follow her example and to put yourself unreservedly in His hands. He is no hard task-master. He is your best friend; He loves you. He knows better than you what is good for you. When your child would come to you, and with the warm affection of a child's heart would tell you, "Mother, I do not want to grieve you again. I will gladly do whatever you tell me," would you test her and put her to the most disagreeable task you can think of? I tell you, I should give her the best day she ever had in her life.

Are you still hesitating? You are thinking of something which has become a habit to you; not exactly a sin, but a weight, something that hinders your growth, your fruitfulness; hinders your giving a joyful testimony to others. The Holy Spirit may perhaps often have put His hand on it, perhaps He is doing so now. F. B. Meyer once taught us a helpful prayer. He told us of something he had not surrendered, something in his life in which he did not let the Lord share, a room which he had kept locked. He said, "I felt unhappy about it. I then prayed, O Lord, make me willing to become willing!" He did.

Your burnt-offering must be without blemish. Christ's was. He was a lamb without blemish. But you say,

"My offering can never be like that." Listen, Christ by
making a perfect burnt-offering covers the imperfec-
tions in mine and yours. We were reading this morning
in our family worship Matthew 23: 19: "Whether is
greater, the gift, or *the altar that sanctifieth the gift?*"—
Christ or your burnt-offering? Take courage. Christ
said to His Father in the prayer of intercession (John
17: 19): "*For their sakes* I sanctify myself, that they
also might be sanctified through the truth." "Both he
that sanctifieth and they who are sanctified are *all of
one*: for which cause he is not ashamed to call them
brethren" (Heb. 2: 11).

Your burnt-offering must be a WHOLE *burnt-offering.*
It is the only offering that had to be burnt altogether.
Nothing of it was taken by the priest, it belonged all
to God. The Holy Spirit puts two photographs side by
side. Evidently He wants us to compare them. Acts 5
begins with *but,* which shows that it is connected with
the preceding verses. Joses of Cyprus had a piece of
ground, a field. He wanted to have something in the
Holy City that belonged to him. He was no longer an
alien. But the need of the church was great, so he sold
his beloved field and laid the money at the apostle's feet.

Ananias and Sapphira had an estate. They *kept back
part of the price*; they brought a certain part. They
lied to the Holy Spirit; they lost their testimony. I do
not know whether they were converted. I trust they
were. If so they came to Christ with a lie on their lips.
I suppose the church in Jerusalem had a treasurer who
entered the gifts in his ledger. No doubt he considered
Ananias was the larger giver. It might have been entered in three or four ciphers. Our Lord reckons differ-

ently. He sat against the treasury. He always does. He said the widow who gave her two mites had cast in more than the others. Our Lord looks not at what we give, but what we keep back. The widow gave all she had. Our Lord looks not at your cheque-book, but at your bank-book. Why do so many missionary societies have a want of funds? Why is there so little spiritual life in many churches? There is a lack of surrender. Barnabas brought a burnt-offering; Ananias did not.

The lamb had to die. It is only through the gate of death that we enter into the full life. Die unto self, live unto Christ. "Except a grain of wheat fall into the ground and die, it abideth alone: but if it die, it bringeth forth much fruit" (John 12: 24). Do you want to bear much fruit? You must die to self. The cross covers your sins, but it does more; it also wants to cover your old self-life. S. D. Gordon, a dear friend of mine, said in one of his books: "If self is on the throne, Christ is on the cross. When the self-life is on the cross, Christ is on the throne."

> Dying with Jesus, by death reckoned mine;
> Living with Jesus, a new life divine;
> Looking to Jesus till glory doth shine,
> Moment by moment, O Lord, I am Thine.

"I am crucified with Christ: nevertheless I live; yet not I, but *Christ liveth in me*: and the life which I now live in the flesh *I live by the faith of the Son of God,* who loved me, and gave himself *for me*" (Gal. 2: 20). Christ gave Himself for you. Should you not give yourself to Him? Everything for everything! He gave all for you. Will you give all to Him? Remember: surrender, consecration does not convey ownership. You are

His already; you are bought with a price. Will you keep back *part of the price*? Are you willing to become a burnt-offering?

> Have Thine own way, Lord!
> Have Thine own way,
> Thou art the potter;
> I am the clay.

I was a young clergyman. In a little village lived a clergyman's widow. She had two sons at college. Both were converted. There was much spiritual life in the college, and missionary interest. John, the eldest, felt called to the mission field, to the west coast of Africa. It was at that time called the white man's grave. When he came home, he asked the old vicar to ask his mother if she would let him go. The old clergyman hardly liked to do it; he thought there were others who might go instead. He went to the home. The old lady in her neat widow's cap came into the little drawing-room. He told her John's wish. "John is a good boy," he said, "he will not go if you do not give your consent." What was her answer? "Sir, before John was born, my dear husband and I gave him to the Lord and prayed the Lord might use him." John went. He was only there nine months. He had not mastered the language yet, but his life was a living testimony. Then came a cable to Salisbury Square, the office of the Church Missionary Society, that God had called His young servant home.

Next Christmas, Willy told the old vicar that he had heard the call from the mission field. He wanted to be his brother's substitute. This time the old vicar shook his head most energetically. Yet he went and told the mother and again said, "Willy is a fine boy, he will never go if you want to keep him." The mother was a moment silent, and then with tears in her eyes and smiling through the tears, she repeated:

> Were the whole realm of nature mine,
>   That were a present far too small;
> Love so amazing, so divine,
>   Demands my life, my soul, my all!

That mother was a burnt-offering. Are you? She kept nothing back. She laid her all upon the altar, and the altar sanctified the gift.

That mother was a whole burnt-offering. Like another widow, she cast into the treasury all she had (Mark 12: 14). Our Lord still sits over against the treasury and beholds what we give and what we hold back. Is our best too good for Him, who gave all for us?

> Laid on Thine altar, O my Lord divine,
>   Accept this gift today for Jesus' sake.
> I have no jewels to adorn Thy shrine
>   Nor any world-famed sacrifice to make;
> But here I bring within my trembling hand
>   *This will of mine*—a thing that seemeth small,
> And Thou alone, O Lord, canst understand
>   How, when I yield Thee this, *I yield Thee all.*
>
> Take it, O Father, ere my courage fail,
>   And merge it so in Thine, that e'en
> If in some desperate hour, my cries prevail
>   And Thou give back my gift, it may have been
> So changed, so purified, so fair have grown,
>   So one with Thee, so filled with peace divine,
> I may not know or feel it as my own
>   But, giving back my will, may find it Thine.
>   —*Selected*

8

THE FIRE WHICH MUST EVER BE BURNING

12. And the fire upon the altar shall be burning in it; it shall *not be put out*: and the priest shall burn wood on it every morning, and lay the burnt-offering in order upon it; and he shall burn thereon the *fat of the peace-offerings.*
13. The fire shall ever be burning upon the altar; it shall *never go out.*—LEVITICUS 6: 12, 13

As a boy I was brought up in a little country-town in Holland. It was about twenty miles from the nearest railway-station. When I was about twelve a most important event happened in our town. A councillor more energetic than others suggested the town should be connected with the nearest railway-station by a little local train. There was much opposition. The farmers were afraid their horses would shy when such a clamping monster met them on the road. At last, after many deliberations, to the great joy of us boys, he carried his proposal.

We boys could hardly await the time when the rails would be laid and the first train would leave the little station. I still remember how the important persons of the town took their seats in the car drawn by a little steam engine. The first few months it was most interesting to travel by it. There was something of adventure in the journey. You could never be quite sure when you would arrive at your destination. One morning it was stopping on the market-place at 11.30, just when the boys were coming out of school. The young machinist could not make it budge. Of course, we boys were interested and ready to proffer suggestions. One, more daring than the rest, suggested, "Perhaps there is no water in the boiler." The machinist, exasperated, threw his wooden shoe at him and said, "*Water enough, but it does not boil.*" The statement has clung to me throughout my ministry. Water enough; we have plenty of organizations in our churches. Ministers able to organize are eagerly sought. We are over-organized. The difficulty is the fire does not burn, the fire of the Holy Ghost.

We once crossed by the Canadian and Pacific to Montreal. In the distance we saw some icebergs—it is a beautiful sight. The captain, however, did not seem to like them. He made a large detour. I have been in churches where I felt inclined to put on an overcoat; the atmosphere was so frigid. I have also at times met Christians who reminded me of icebergs. When the risen Lord joined the two disciples on the way to Emmaus and opened to them the Scriptures, their hearts began to burn. "Did not our heart burn within us while he talked with us by the way?" (Luke 24 : 32). The Lord does not like lukewarm hearts. What we need in our churches and on the mission field is Christians with a burning heart. Sister Eve of Friedenshort had a motto on the wall of her room : "Blessed are the burning ones, for they will conquer the world for Jesus Christ."

The burnt-offering has been slain, its blood is sprinkled on the altar, its fat burnt on the altar, a type of the perfect sinlessness of our Lord even when He was bearing the load of our sins on the cross, a type of His perfect obedience and harmony with the will of His heavenly Father throughout His life. He was the only man who could say: "I do *always* those *things that please him*" (John 8: 29). He did so during His agony in those dark hours on the cross. The fat offered on the altar—in His life as in His death—Christ was an odour of a sweet smell, a sacrifice acceptable, well-pleasing to God.

We now leave the altar and court. A solemn procession carries forth the offering "without the camp into a clean place, where the ashes are poured out, and burn him on the wood with fire" (Lev. 4: 12). Let us watch that burning in silence. I do not wish to add any words of my own. "They took Jesus, and led him away. And he bearing his cross went forth into a place called the place of a skull, which is called in the Hebrew Golgotha: where they crucified him" (John 19: 16–18).

"The bodies of those beasts, whose blood is brought into the sanctuary by the high priest for sin, are burned without the camp. Wherefore Jesus also, that he might *sanctify* the people with his own blood, suffered without the gate. Let us go forth therefore unto him *without the camp, bearing his reproach*" (Heb. 13: 11–13).

Without the camp—sanctification and separation go together. "Be ye *not conformed to this world*: but be ye transformed." Not con, but trans. In the world, but not of the world. The ship in the water, but not the water in the ship.

The fire shall not go out. That fire was not lit by human hands. It could not. "The fire came out *from before the Lord*, and consumed upon the altar the burnt-offering and the fat: which when all the people *saw,* they *shouted* and fell on their faces" (Lev. 9: 24). The word Evangelist is an honoured word; it is Scriptural. You do not find the word *revivalist* in the Bible. A real revival is not man-made; the fire must come from heaven. The Baptist said: "I indeed *baptize you with water* unto repentance, but he that cometh after me is mightier than I, whose shoes I am not worthy to bear: HE shall baptize you with the *Holy Ghost,* and *with fire."* The *fullness of the Holy Spirit,* a baptism with fire—that is what you and I need. Without it, it is impossible to do efficient service. Andrew Murray wrote in 1895: "It is the will of God that *every* child of God should be *filled* with the Holy Spirit. Without this fullness no child of God can either live or work according to Father's ideals."

Let us stand and watch the fire as it burns to ashes the burnt-offering. We shall find that the fire cleanses, fire transforms, fire spreads.

Fire cleanses. God's summons to Israel when they returned from the Babylonian captivity was: "Be ye clean, that bear the vessels of the Lord" (Isa. 52: 11). His servants should have clean hands. David prayed: "*Create* in me a clean heart, and renew a right spirit within me" (Ps. 51: 10).

Fire will *reveal* the nature of our life's work. The great day, when God's children shall stand before the judgment seat of Christ, when He comes and brings His rewards with Him, shall declare the nature of our life's work, what sort it is, whether it be gold, silver, precious stones, or wood, hay, stubble. Many a house that looks so grand to us will turn out after all to be hay and stubble. Only that which is done from love to the Master, to His Honour, not ours, will have abiding value (1 Cor. 3: 12–15). Brother minister, let us watch the fire burning the offering! Let it warn you and me.

Fire transfigures. "He shall sit as a refiner and purifier of silver: and he shall purify the sons of Levi . . . *then* shall the offering of Judah and Jerusalem be pleasant unto the Lord" (Mal. 3: 3, 4). Do not shun the refining fire. Are you in the refining fire just now? Brother, do not fear it, rather thank God for it. It shows at least that you are silver and that God thinks you are capable of rendering better service for Him after you have passed through the fire. That is the reason why He takes so much pains with you.

Your heavenly Father, who loves you with an everlasting love, is Himself the refiner. He *sits* and watches the fire. He takes care that the fire is not too hot. He will not leave you too long in the fire. Silversmiths speak of the silver look. As soon as the scum, the murmuring, the self-seeking has gone; as soon as His face is reflected in the silver, He Himself will take you out of the fire, a *vessel* meet for the Master's use.

When we cease looking at ourselves, when we are willing to raise the veil covering our face, when with open face we behold His glory, then we shall reflect it and be changed from character to character by the Holy Spirit (2 Cor. 3: 18). Then too will others, even our antagonists, take notice that we have been in the school of Jesus. Yes, the fire transfigures. "If *any man* [whatever his past, by whatever sins he is enthralled, if he be the greatest sinner in the town] *be in Christ,* he is a new *creature*: *old things* are passed away; behold, all things are become new" (2 Cor. 5: 17).

Fire spreads. It is the nature of fire. Do you not long for the fire to spread? Do you not wish for a revival, sinners to be saved, saints built up in the faith before the Lord comes? As we watch the fire consuming the offering, let me teach you a prayer: "Lord, give us a revival and begin with me."

Have you ever asked yourselves what was the cause that Christianity spread so quickly in so short a time, that in less than thirty years after Christ's death the good news was spread all over the then known world? Study the Acts of the Apostles or if you like the Acts of the Holy Ghost. Again and again we read: "They were *all filled* with the Holy Ghost." The Holy Spirit glorifies Jesus. He does not speak of Himself; He speaks of Jesus. He keeps reminding us of Jesus and His words. The heart becomes so full of Jesus that even when threatened to keep silent, the apostles said: "We cannot but speak the things which we have seen and heard" (Acts. 4: 20).

Fire spreads. "Believers were the more added to the Lord, *multitudes* both of *men* and women" (Acts 5: 14). Brother minister, would you not long for the Holy Spirit to give this testimony to your town? Think of it, *multitudes* and not only women, *but* men also. The good news itself, but also the messengers who brought it, must have exercised a great attractive power. Yes, you say, but that was in the early church. Quite right, but is not the same Holy Spirit able and willing to endue with the same power men and women willing to yield themselves entirely to His control?

Fire spreads. The early church knew what persecution was. It cost something to follow Christ out of the camp, to hear His reproach. Saul made havoc of the church, throwing men and women into prison. They were forced to leave Jerusalem, their birthplace. I mean the place of their new birth. You say, "What a pity!" Oh, no. "They that were scattered abroad went everywhere preaching the gospel" (Acts 8: 3, 4). You say, "Yes, but they were apostles." You are wrong there. They were simple every-day folk. The apostles remained in Jerusalem. The reason: every member of the church was a missionary, *they were all filled with the Holy Ghost.* They had a burning heart. They were fire-flames, and fire spreads.

Dear friends, I am loath to leave the brazen altar and to pass on to the other vessels of the tabernacle. The Lord has been speaking to me at that altar. I hope He has to you. Before passing on, let me give you some simple rules about keeping up a good fire.

The fire shall not go out. I do not know how your fire burns, whether it gives good heat. You know. The apostle warned a young preacher, who was his dearly beloved son and his fellow-servant in Jesus Christ, to "*stir up* the gift of God, which is in thee by the putting on of Paul's hands" (2 Tim. 1: 6). The word "stir up" is significant, to put new life into the fire. It seemed to burn rather low; the flame had died down. Power was lacking; it needed reviving. Reader, what about your fire?

Take up the ashes which the fire has consumed with the burnt-offering on the altar. This is the first rule to get a good fire. Ashes keep down the flame. You will never get a bright fire where there is accumulation of ashes.

Note that these ashes were the result of the burning of the burnt-offering. You have preached a powerful sermon. God has blessed it. There were decisions made for Christ. You have been speaking at a conference. God's children have had a new vision of Christ and of a victory in daily life, of the fullness of the Holy Spirit. "Non nobis, non nobis." All the praise and the glory be His. Brother, beware of the ashes. After every service I have to ask my beloved Master to cover with His precious blood whatever there was done or spoken in the flesh and not in the Spirit.

Remove the ashes. I held a series of gospel meetings. The pastor and many of God's children had been praying for showers of blessing. Much prayer, and yet showers did not come, only single drops. One evening in my address, I was led to quote the Lord's words (Matt. 5: 23), "Therefore if *thou bring thy gift* to the altar and there remembereth that thy brother hath ought against thee; leave there thy gift before the altar, and go thy way; first be reconciled to thy brother, and then come and offer thy gift." In the middle of the address one of the elders rose from his place and went into the vestry. I wondered if I had said something which had upset him. The elders there are supposed to be sermon-tasters. My consternation grew considerably after a little time when a second elder left and went into the vestry. After a short time they came back and took their seats again with beaming faces. That evening the clouds broke, and up till the close we had continuous blessing. Why did those elders leave the church? For a considerable time they had a grudge against each other, avoiding each other, and did not speak to each other. In the vestry they confessed their faults to God and to each other, and with a relieved heart they shook hands. The ashes had been removed and the flames went high.

May I ask you tenderly, have any ashes been accumulating with you? Would you like to be the cause that hindered the Holy Spirit of pouring His blessing on your church? May the Lord show us the ashes and make us willing to obey our Lord and to make right where we have wronged somebody in word or deed. When the ashes are removed, the fire will burn.

And the priest shall burn wood upon the altar every morning. This second rule seems also self-evident. How can a fire burn if there is no fuel put on it? The fuel you and I need is the daily reading of God's Word for our own souls. I do not refer here to systematic study of the Bible. Every minister would, I take it, devote part of his morning to this. Neither do I refer here to your family-prayers. I take it you have a family altar and read daily with your children the Word of God. I praise the Lord that in my parents' home no meal was taken without the reading of God's Word. My parents believed this to be according to Scripture. "Every creature of God is good, and nothing to be refused, if it be received with thanksgiving: for *it is sanctified by the Word of God and prayer*" (1 Tim. 4: 4, 5).

Wood on your own fire, food for your own soul—with the Bible in the closet. When you pray, you speak to Father. When you read, Father speaks to you. The danger with us preachers is—at least with me—that so often when I read of a striking passage in God's Word I am thinking how to use it in the next sermon or Bible-reading. I must first be fed before I can feed others. Oh, how I do want daily food myself.

Wood in the morning. It is a general rule in most houses, I take it, to lay the fire in the morning. Wood is fine fuel. I have had occasion to observe that in Florida. Will you forgive my adding that *paper is not*? There are some fine daily papers, some with thirty-two pages and even more, but if you devote your morning hour to studying the daily paper till you have come to the advertisements, instead of going to the reading of God's Word, you will find that your fire will gradually die down.

Wood in the morning. Give the first part of your day to God and fellowship with Him. Speak to Him, but give Him also an opportunity to speak to you. Take fresh wood each day. The Gibeonites brought stale bread; let your bread be fresh. Even in reading our Bibles we are liable to get in a groove. I once heard Dr. Griffith Thomas giving excellent advice to his students in Oxford. He said, "Use at least two Bibles, one of which you underline every word that has become valuable to you; but when you go into your closet, take a Bible in which you make no marking or underlining so that the Holy Spirit can open up to you a fresh passage each day." Excellent advice I found it.

He shall burn thereon the fat of the peace-offering. Of course, fat will make the fire burn. We have so much to thank God for. I had a dear friend, now in glory, who, when he met somebody in the early morning, his regular question was: "Have you something to thank

God for?" "Bless the Lord, O my soul, and *forget not all his benefits.*" When at a Bible conference the hymn was suggested: "Count you many blessings, name them one by one, and it will surprise you what the Lord has done." A dear friend of mine now in glory, Dr. White, said if he had to do that somebody would have to make him a present of an adding machine.

May the Lord give you and me a grateful spirit. "We beseech thee, give us that due sense of all thy mercies, that our hearts may be unfeignedly thankful, and that we show forth thy praise, not only with our lips, but in our lives; by giving up ourselves to thy service, and by walking before thee in holiness and righteousness all our day; through Jesus Christ our Lord to whom with thee and the Holy Ghost be all honour and glory, world without end, Amen."

The Laver of Brass

9

THE LAVER OF BRASS AND CLEANSING

17. And the Lord spake unto Moses, saying,
18. Thou shalt also make a laver of brass, to *wash* withal: and thou shalt put it between the tabernacle of the congregation and the altar, and thou shalt put *water* therein.
19. For Aaron and his sons shall *wash* their *hands* and their *feet* thereat:
20. When they go into the tabernacle of the congregation, *that they die not.*—EXODUS 30: 17–20

EVERY morning our little twins had a fresh pinafore. As mother knew her twins, she told them to be careful and not dirty themselves. It is remarkable what an attraction dirt has for children. When it had been raining during the night and there were plenty of little waterpools, how they loved to jump about in them. It did not take long before one of them fell—the fresh apron, hands and face all dirty.

The little sinner goes repenting to mother and asks her not to be angry. She kisses away the tears; mothers know how to do that. He knows he is forgiven. And then he has to go about with dirty hands and face and dirty pinafore? Oh, no. She not only forgives, she washes face and hands and puts a fresh pinafore on. Is that all? There is something better than a clean pinafore. If only I could have given my boys a disposition to hate dirt and dislike jumping in pools they would have avoided a good deal of their troubles.

We are big children of our heavenly Father. "Father Himself *loves* you," the Lord Jesus said (John 16: 27). At the brazen altar He has taken away my filthy rags (Isa. 64: 6), and "hath clothed me with the garments of salvation, he hath covered me with the robe of righteousness" (Isa. 61: 10). Father too would like to see His children always clean. "Let thy garments be *always white*; and let thy head lack no ointment" (Eccles. 9: 8).

At the brazen altar we received a new nature. "Being born again, not of corruptible seed, but of incorruptible, by *the word of God*, which liveth and abideth for ever" (1 Pet. 1: 23). Our old nature loves dirt; our new nature detests it. There is a constant struggle between the two; which of them shall be the master. Too often our old nature has the victory. They are Christians, but carnal Christians, babes in Christ. Of course, this is not Father's intention. He likes His children to grow in stature. "He sent his son that we might have life and have it more abundantly." Unfortunately many of God's children never go farther than the brazen altar.

God commanded Moses to build a laver of brass. It was to stand midway between the altar and the door of the tabernacle. God provided the means for cleansing from the defilement of sin. In it the priest was to wash his hands and feet before he was allowed to serve God in the sanctuary. Certainly he washed completely his whole body before entering the court, but passing from the altar his feet had come in contact with the earth, and whatever touches the earth becomes soiled. No priest was allowed to enter the sanctuary with unclean feet or hands. If he did, he was put to death.

The Babylonian captivity had come to an end. The

Lord had redeemed His people. He did not want them to remain in Babylon even though it would be possible to amass large fortunes by the world's trade. This was not God's thought for His people: "Depart ye, depart ye, go ye out from thence, touch no unclean thing; go ye out of the midst of her; *be ye clean, that bear the vessels of the Lord*" (Isa. 52: 11).

In God's plan justification should be followed by *sanctification*. Altar and laver are inseparable companions. At the brazen altar by the blood our guilt is cancelled, at the laver the defilement of sin is washed away. "*Without shedding* of blood there is *no remission*" (Heb. 9: 22). "*Without holiness* no man shall see the Lord" (Heb. 12: 14). Sin is trespassing, going where you are not allowed to go. It is transgression, stepping over the right path, iniquity, unjust dealing with God, as well as a disease spreading its germs everywhere, it is uncleanness; it is *dirt*. If you come in contact with dirt, you become *dirty*. When your boy comes to the table with a clean face but dirty hands, you would say, "Dirty boy." Our Father not only forgives, but He also cleanseth. One of the most precious words in the Bible is 1 John 1: 9. It shows us the only way for a child of God, mentioned in God's Word, to be restored to communion. "If *we confess* our sins, he is faithful and just to *forgive* us our sins, and to *cleanse* us from *all* unrighteousness." God promises not only forgiveness, but also cleansing. He provides not the brazen altar only, but also the laver.

"But *if we walk* in the light, as he is in the light, we have fellowship one with another, and the *blood* of Jesus Christ his Son *cleanseth* us from all sin" (1 John

1: 7). Cleansing through the blood is not the same as forgiveness through the blood. Forgiveness comprehends the whole load of our sins, sins in our past, sins in the present, even sins we are still going to do in the future. They are all covered by the blood. The Lord be praised for the brazen altar.

Cleansing through the blood refers to the individual sin. God forgives sins; He cleanses from sin, from every sin. The Holy Spirit is associated with the cleansing. "But ye are *washed*, but ye are sanctified, but *ye are justified* in the name of the Lord Jesus, and by the Spirit of our God" (1 Cor. 6: 11). God the Holy Ghost, who sanctifieth me and all the elect people of God, cleanseth from every sin. If you wish to be cleansed, you must pray the Holy Spirit to show you every single sin in His light. The Holy Spirit will answer your prayer; He will find the right time and the right opportunity to deal with it.

There is certainly a condition. We must walk (be living) in the light, not in the light of your assembly, not in the light of a brother to whom you look up, but in *His* light. Ask the Lord what He thinks, not only of your actions or words, but about the motive or disposition which is behind it. It is not the manifestation of the sin, not the symptoms of the disease, but the sin itself, the sinful disposition which is important. John says: "If we walk in the light, as *He is in the light.*" God is continuously in the light. He is "the Father of lights, with whom is no *variableness*, neither shadow of turning" (Jas. 1: 17). If you long to experience the cleansing power of the blood, you cannot live one week in the light and the next week in darkness. If you do, you may have the forgiving power of the blood, never its cleansing power.

"There is a fountain filled with blood, drawn from Immanuel's veins." The Lord be praised that we may go to that fountain and find forgiveness, but we should not stop there. The forgiveness of the sin should be followed by the cleansing, otherwise we might perhaps have to come next week and ask forgiveness again for committing the same sin. When you have seen that sin in His light and what it means for God and for you, you will not be satisfied with forgiveness, but you will pass on to the laver of brass.

Cleansing from every sin. Is this possible? It is through the cleansing by the blood. Notice John does not say through Jesus' blood, but through the blood of *Jesus Christ, His Son.* There is power, wonderful power in the blood of the Lamb. This is what He wants you to feel. The blood which cleanses us from every sin is the blood of *Jesus Christ, the Son of God.*

As we stand with folded hands at the laver of brass, may I pray with you a prayer that the church has prayed for many centuries: "Almighty God, unto whom all hearts be open, all desires known, and from whom no secrets are hid; cleanse the thoughts of our hearts by the inspiration of thy Holy Spirit, that we may perfectly love thee, and worthily magnify thy holy Name; through Jesus Christ our Lord. Amen."

10

THE LAVER OF BRASS AND THE LOOKING-GLASS

8 And he made the laver of *brass,* and the foot of
it of brass of the *looking-glasses* of the *women assem-*
bling, which assembled *at the door* of the tabernacle
of the congregation.—EXODUS 38: 8

I AM not surprised that many good women had assembled at the door of the tabernacle. They generally
form the majority in our congregations now. I am glad
though that the Holy Spirit draws our attention to it
in the Old Testament. The world does not recognize
what it owes good women. Women were the last at the
cross and the first at the grave. It was a woman who,
through her joyful testimony of the Lord, had living
water to give and drew a whole town to the feet of the
Saviour. It was a woman who, more than any of the
apostles, showed a deep understanding for the Lord's
mission, and to whom the Lord gave that desirable
praise: "She has done what she could." No, I am not
surprised that they were attracted to the door of the
congregation.

And, of course, they wanted their share in offering
their gifts to God. And again, I am not surprised.
Women are more liberal than men any day. They like
giving. I cannot help smiling when their thoughts fastened on looking-glasses. They had been given them

by the Egyptian women. They were wonderful speci-
mens of Egyptian handicraft. They were of brass and
were highly polished—quite equals of the best modern
mirrors. God had said the laver had to be made of
brass; it seemed natural to them that they should bring
the only brass in their possession, their looking-glasses.

Many years ago my wife and I visited the famous
palace of Sanssouci at Versailles. We paused a little in
the private royal apartments and thought of the sad fate
of the weak king, Louis XVI, and his beautiful wife.

The guide led us into the hall of mirrors. All the
walls were covered with the most costly mirrors. With
a smile the guide pointed out to us a large looking-
glass in the corner. If you looked at it from one side
you could hardly recognize yourself. All the little spots
and wrinkles you never had noticed were magnified. In
fact, you hardly saw anything but spots and failures.
It was rather discouraging. To comfort us, he had us
look at the other side. We saw ourselves in the best
possible light, the spots and failures had disappeared.
We were rather gratified. He told us Marie Antoinette
liked to spend some time in the hall of mirrors. At which
side of the mirror she preferred to look he did not know.

It seems that many of God's children have a mirror
room and like to look at their own picture from the best
side. They know many others who do less for the Lord
and give less for the Lord's work than they. They are
ready to give themselves a good testimonial. It is remarkable how little perspective some of God's children
have. They have a different standard for themselves
than for their brothers and sisters in Christ. They put
them in the bad corner of the mirror room and see their

failings with a magnifying glass. They see the mote in the brother's eye, but not the beam in their own. What a harm a spirit of criticism does in our gatherings; what a harm we do to ourselves and others. It is like cancer and wormwood. It keeps back conversions; it hinders our own growth; it grieves our loving Saviour who had such a keen eye for the good in others and who has warned us: "Judge not that ye be not judged. With what measure ye mete, it shall be measured to you again" (Matt. 7: 1, 2). Remember, we are prone to see those failures in others which we have ourselves. They look heinous in others; we excuse them in ourselves. David may have had many excuses for his sinful deed with Bathsheba, but when Nathan showed him its heinousness in another, he was ready with the judgment. "As the Lord liveth, the man that hath done this thing shall surely die" (2 Sam. 12: 5). There is a danger in looking-glasses. I am glad the good women put theirs in the clever hands of Bezaleel to make out of them a laver of brass.

Aaron and his sons shall wash their hands and their hands and their feet thereat. The laver is for God's children, not for the unconverted. Water cannot regenerate anybody. The laver is not for sins before conversion, but for sin after conversion. Sins of His own hurt the Saviour far more than sins of the worldly. If your children wrong you, that hurts you far more than if a stranger does it. One of the most pathetic verses in the Bible is, "He came to his own, and they received him not." "And one shall say unto him: What are these wounds in thy hand? Then he shall answer: Those with which I was wounded in *the house of my friends*." Those are the wounds that sting, that break the heart. Peter hurt the Lord more than the servant of the high priest, that smote His face. Sin is a hateful thing, it is evidence of black ingratitude. You know the story of the noble lady who threw herself at Cromwell's feet and begged him to spare her husband's life. The answer of the man with the iron heart was, "A man, a man; a word, a word. When the vesper clock from the tower strikes six, your husband's head shall fall." The scaffold was erected in the market place. Soldiers led the prisoner to the scaffold. His head was on the block. The executioner stood with drawn sword awaiting the stroke of the clock. The sun was going down blood-red. The people were waiting in dead silence. The clock did not strike. "An oracle, an oracle," the crowd cried. "Spare his life!" The officer and the soldiers went to the tower. The verger was tolling, pulling hard; frightened sweat was on his forehead. The officer mounted the steps to the steeple. There the brave woman with both hands was clinging to the clapper as it was striking the bell. She fell down in a swoon, the flesh torn from the crushed hands. She had saved her husband's life. The iron man said, "A man, a man; a word, a word. The clock did not strike, her husband's life is spared."

I want to ask you a question. When that husband was sitting at his dinner-table, looking at those crushed hands on the opposite side, could ever a harsh word against her pass his lips? As we stand at the laver, let us ask our Lord to cleanse us not only from sin but from the love of sin. Your Saviour did more for you than that noble woman did for her husband.

Let us not play with sin. Eve did: she looked, she

saw, she ate, and she gave. Those are the four steps downwards. It is not the *first* look. You often cannot help it. It is the second, the third look. Psychology will tell you that the moment comes when you are no longer able to resist. Eve had eaten the apple long before it touched her lips. Many a servant of the Lord has in a weak moment spoiled a life of useful service, but the fall had begun long before. He had been playing with sin. Job made a covenant with his eyes. Will you do it too? (Job 31: 1).

When the heart is full of Jesus, and realizes what Christ has suffered for him, then there is not room for the love of sin. When your surrender to Christ is not entire, when you do not surrender to Him your whole life, remember, what you keep back does not belong to you, it belongs to Satan. Drummond spoke of the propelling force of a new affection. He meant love to Christ drives out the love to sin. At the laver we learn that love to sin, however hidden it may be in our hearts, is already uncleanness.

The Lord expects His children to have *clean hands*. "Who shall ascend into the hill of the Lord? He that hath *clean hands, and a pure heart*" (Ps. 24: 3, 4). You cannot serve the Lord with unclean hands. If your hands are unclean, wash them at once; do not wait till the evening. When the Holy Spirit convicts you of having sinned, go immediately to the Lord and confess your sin. Ask Him to cleanse you. If you put it off, you will lose your joy, you will neglect the study of the Word, you will be backsliding. In nine cases out of ten, backsliding begins with the neglect of the Word. Your prayer life will suffer, you will be no longer keen to win others for the Lord. Dr. Torrey used to counsel new converts to keep short accounts with the Lord. It was good advice. Only with clean hands and clean feet you can have fellowship with the Lord in the sanctuary. "Draw nigh to God, and he will draw nigh to you. Cleanse your hands, ye sinners; and purify your hearts, ye double-minded" (Jas. 4: 8).

I want you to make a mental picture: it is the upper room, Christ being with His disciples His last evening on earth. He is going to eat the Passover with them. He knew that the hour had come that He should depart to the Father. He knew, too, that the way to Father would go over Gethsemane, Pilate's Praetorium, and Golgotha. He knew it all. I want you to watch the Lord as He goes from one to another taking the towel and stooping to wash His disciples' feet. Do you follow Him? Do you know who the man is before whom He is stooping now? It is Peter. He objects. The Lord tells him that unless He washes Peter's feet, he had no part with him. Do you long to bring others to Christ?

Clean feet, clean hands, *a pure heart*. The Lord knew the human heart. He knew what proceeded out of the heart. What about the hidden motives of our actions? Jesus said, "I seek not my own glory." Does not "self" protrude in our service for the Master? A pure heart seeks only the glory of Jesus. What *about your thought-life*? That is a secret between you and God. No one else knows of it. Do you ever make mental pictures which you would not like your mother to see? Do not say that there is no harm in thoughts. Psychopathology will tell you that the effect of sinful thoughts may be more injurious than sinful deeds. Ezekiel had a sad vision of profanation of the temple. He tells us of the seventy ancients and of their chambers of imagery. Every form of creeping things and abominable beasts, and all the idols of the house of Israel were portrayed upon the wall round about (Ezek. 8: 10). Our Lord knew the thoughts of the scribes (Matt. 9: 4), but He also knows ours: "The Lord knoweth the thoughts of man, that they are vanity" (Ps. 94: 11).

The heart, Evan Hopkins says, is the central region of our being where three things are focused: the thoughts, the desires, and the will. Everyone is constantly thinking and desiring and willing; and the nature and current of his thoughts, the character and aim of his desires, as well as the attitude and direction of his will, determine the state of his heart. The man who by God's grace is regenerated has received a new nature and cannot become unregenerate though he may degenerate. But his heart may change from day to day. Today the Lord's beatitude may belong to him—"Blessed are the pure in heart"; tomorrow he may relapse into sin and lose that blessing. Now it is our privilege and our duty to be cleansed in thought and in desire, to be brought in a condition of loyalty in will and purpose, and to be kept in this state of conformity to Christ, moment by moment. "Faithful is he who hath called us, who also will do it." And the heart which the Lord cleanses He also fills.

We have paused a long time before the laver. For many it has been a solemn hour. We have seen that hands and feet are unclean; that some sin had obtained a power over us because we secretly loved it; that we often have sought our own honour and sought praise of men, instead of waiting for the "Well done" from the lips of the Master. With the leper we had to cry: "Unclean and unclean." We cannot clean ourselves; we could not convert ourselves—we have tried it. And we cannot sanctify ourselves—we have tried that too. But what we cannot do, God the Holy Spirit is waiting to do for us.

Thou shalt put water therein (Exod. 40: 7). The laver itself cannot cleanse us. It is the water that cleanses. God gave water for cleansing, the blood for forgiveness. "According to his mercy he saved us, by the *washing of regeneration*, and renewing of the Holy Ghost" (Titus 3: 5). "Christ loved the church, and gave himself for it; that he might *sanctify* and *cleanse* it with the washing of water *by the word*" (Eph. 5: 25, 26). Our Lord prays, "Sanctify them through thy truth: *thy word is truth*" (John 17: 17).

It will be clear to the reader that the cleansing water is a symbol of the Word, of the living Word, the risen Saviour in the Word. Purposely I have let the Word speak in these talks. I hope that the readers will meditate on the words I have quoted. There is more power in the Word than in any human explanation.

I said above, the water is for cleansing, the blood for forgiveness. I do not want you to infer from this that two fountains have been given us: one for forgiveness, the other for cleansing. Water and blood in God's Word are closely joined together. The unclean person was cleansed by the sprinkling with running water, but in the water were the ashes of the red heifer (Num. 19: 17). Of our blessed Lord, John said: "This is he that *came by water and blood*, even Jesus Christ; not by water only, but by water and blood. And it is the Spirit that

beareth witness, because the Spirit is truth" (1 John
5: 6). "But one of the soldiers with a spear pierced his
side, and forthwith came there out *blood and water*"
(John 19: 34).

We cannot clease ourselves, but God can. He promised it to Israel after He had taken them from among
the nations and brought them back into their own land.
What the Lord promised to Israel, He also promises to
them who by faith are the children of Abraham. If you
have given up the hope of ever becoming clean, take
hold of the promise: "*I will* sprinkle *clean water* upon
you, and ye *shall be clean*: from *all* your filthiness, and
from *all* your idols, will *I* cleanse you. A *new heart* also
will *I give you,* and a new spirit will I put within you:
and *I* will take away the stony heart out of your flesh,
and *I will give you* an heart of flesh. And *I* will put my
spirit within you, and *I will cause you* to walk in my
statutes, and ye shall keep my judgments, and do them"
(Ezek. 36: 25–27). I need not add a word nor detract
a word. I believe that God means what He says. We
like to see something and to feel something. God says
nothing about feeling. We walk by faith, not by sight.
He does not say anything about what you have to do; it
is all about what *He* is going to do. The Lord said: "*I
will give.*" Cleansing and *Sanctification* is a *gift* as well
as Salvation. A gift must be given; a gift must be
accepted; a gift must be used. It is faith that takes the
divine hand which offers the gift. "And God, which
knoweth the hearts, bare them witness, *giving* them
(that means us Gentiles, we that were afar off) the
Holy Ghost, even as he did unto us; and put no difference between us and them, purifying their hearts BY

FAITH" (Acts 15: 8, 9). The life of a Christian is a *walk of faith*. "*As* ye have received Christ Jesus the Lord, *so walk ye in him*" (Col. 2: 6). By faith we accepted our Lord as our Saviour, who bore the punishment of our sin; by faith we accept Him as our *Cleanser* through water and blood.

How the process of cleansing is taking place, I cannot tell you because it is an *inward process*. Trust the Lord Jesus for your cleansing and trust Him for keeping you clean; and He is able and willing to do so when you abide in Him, when you can say with Paul: "I live, yet not I but *Christ liveth in me*." Christ in us the hope of glory and of cleansing. It is all in Christ, nothing apart from Him.

Let me make this clear through an illustration. I well remember the time when there was no gas, no electricity. I am going to tell you something which is an impossibility. Here is a room pitch dark; you cannot feel your way in it. (I was going to say you feel the darkness.) Now I am coming with a brightly burning lamp into your dark room. I put so much light into the room that the room is now full of light and remains light. It does not require the lamp any more.

Now let us use the same illustration once more, but this time there is nothing impossible about it: the darkness in the room signifies sin in our hearts, the lamp our sanctification. What the lamp is for the room, the Lord is for the heart of the believer. By the light of his presence sin is kept without the sphere of our consciousness. Cleanness is not something we have in ourselves, it depends on the indwelling of Christ in the heart. As long as Christ reigns in my heart, the power of sin is broken.

Shall I feel sad because I have nothing in me apart from my Lord? On the contrary, I rejoice that I have to depend altogether on Him and have to *lean hard*. A simple sentence has helped me greatly. Jesus is stronger than the devil. Do you also believe that? Jesus is stronger than temptation. Do you believe that too? Jesus is stronger than my old nature. Do you really believe this?

The laver is the only vessel of the tabernacle of which no dimensions are given in the Bible. There is no limit to the cleansing and keeping power of the Lord Jesus Christ. "Now unto him that is able to *keep you from falling*, and to present you faultless before the presence of his glory with exceeding joy, to the only wise God *our Saviour*, be glory and majesty, dominion and power, both now and ever. Amen" (Jude 24–25).

11

GOLD-GILDED BOARDS ON SILVER SOCKETS

15. And thou shalt make *boards* for the tabernacle of *acacia wood* standing up.

17. Two tenons shall there be in one board, set in order one against another: thus shalt thou make for *all the boards of the tabernacle.*

19. And thou shalt make forty sockets of silver under the twenty boards; *two sockets under one board* for his two tenons.

26. And thou shalt make *bars of acacia wood; five for the boards of the one* side of the tabernacle.

27. And *five bars* for the boards of the *other side.*

28. And the *middle bar* in the midst of the boards shall *reach from end to end.*

29. And thou shalt *overlay the boards with gold,* and make their rings of gold for places for the bars: and thou shalt overlay the bars with gold.

—Exodus 26: 15, 17, 19, 26–29

THE brazen altar and the ark stood at the two extremes of the court. We notice that in Exodus 25–30, the section devoted to the description of the tabernacle, God begins with the ark. Fallen man could not meet God at the ark, but God could meet men at the brazen altar. In the incarnation God came to man in Christ; by the cross man is brought near to God. In incarnation, love, divine love, and truth was manifested in human form and God was manifested in the flesh, and John says: "We beheld his glory (the glory as of the only begotten of the Father), full of grace and truth,"

95

Gold-Gilded Boards on Silver Sockets

but atonement was won, *through the blood* through Christ's death and passion. "By *his own blood Christ* entered in *once* into the holy place, having obtained eternal redemption for us" (Heb. 9:12).

Not without blood. Man may object to the word, but it was the only way by which Christ could consecrate a new and living way to the heart of our Father. Thanks be to God, the vail is rent and we have free access to the throne of grace.

We have seen in a previous chapter that the length of the court was fifty yards and its breadth twenty-five yards. The length of the tabernacle was fifteen yards and the breadth five yards.

The tabernacle was designed by God Himself, and Moses had to make it according to the pattern he saw in the mount. The Holy Spirit shows us in Hebrews 9 that the tabernacle shadows forth the great truth that the way into the Holiest is open, and that in Christ we have our place in the Holiest of holies. The tabernacle is a type of the true one. The Epistle to the Hebrews shows us that it must needs be of a temporary character. It was intended for wilderness use and had to be movable. As long as His people dwelt in tents, God was satisfied to have His habitation in a tent.

God Himself had called by name His servants whom He had honoured to carry out His plans; and when God calls us in His service, He is responsible for our equipment. And so we find that they had been filled "with the Spirit of God, in wisdom, in understanding, and in knowledge, and in all manner of workmanship" (Exod. 31:3). It may perhaps strike some of my readers that the fullness of the Holy Spirit was given them not for preaching nor teaching, but for *all manner of work-manship*. If we would only recognize that, the fullness of the Holy Spirit will help us in whatever work the Lord has entrusted to us; and He will not only help us in doing better work, but make us better men and women.

The readers will like to know the names of those two honoured servants God Himself had chosen for this holy work. I feel sure God had been training them in their youth. Somehow I think that like brother Lawrence they practised the presence of God. Their names are significant. Bezaleel was the man who lived in the shadow of God. Where Bezaleel was, God was. Aholiab was the man who was at home in Father's tent. I do not wonder God could use Bezaleel and Aholiab. Before we commence the study of the tabernacle, let us a moment fold our hands. "O Lord, give me the conscious-ness of Thy presence wherever I am, whatever I do, whatever I say, through Jesus Christ my Lord. Amen."

Let us make a mental picture of the tabernacle. It would be the size of a small hall, fifteen yards long, five yards wide. It was a collapsible tent, four curtains not resting as the tents we are familiar with on a pole, but on a framework of wood. This consisted of forty-eight boards all made of the same material, acacia wood, and overlaid with gold: twenty boards on the south and north sides, six on the west side and two additional ones for the corners. Each board had two tenons fas-tened into solid blocks of silver to keep them standing firmly upright. The sockets were each sixteen inches long, weighing each about an hundredweight and each pair dovetailed together—a silver foundation.

Besides this, to hold the twenty boards together there were five bars: two bars at the top, each going half-way along each side, and in the same way two bars at the bottom; the middle bar going from one end to the other of the sanctuary. These bars were also of acacia wood, overlaid with gold. These bars were fastened to the boards by staples of gold both at the foot and the top.

Having now a clear picture of the framework of the tabernacle—the boards, the sockets, and bars—let us pray the Holy Spirit to show us their spiritual meaning.

Why do I ask you to pray with me? I believe we are treading on holy ground. We shall have to meditate on our Lord. I believe that the tabernacle is a symbol of Christ in His twofold nature—human and divine. I believe that God was in Christ reconciling the world to Himself. I believe also that Christ is the embodiment of the love of the Triune God to a fallen race. I pray that the tabernacle may teach me more of the length and breadth, the depth and height of that love which passeth all understanding.

If the tabernacle is a symbol of Christ, it should also be a type of the church of Christ and its individual members. "We are no more strangers and foreigners, but we are *built* upon the foundation of the apostles and the prophets, *Jesus Christ* himself being the chief corner stone; in whom all the building fitly framed together groweth unto an holy *temple* in the Lord" (Eph. 2: 19–21). The apostle says to each individual member: "Do you not know that ye are the sanctuary of God and that the Holy Spirit has made his home within you?" (1 Cor. 3: 16).

The framework of gilded board shows, therefore, the Ecclesia, the called-out one, the Church of Christ, as she is in Christ. We cannot separate the body from the head, which is Christ. Augustine has already pointed this out when he said, "Totus Christus caput et corpus est." "The whole Christ is head and body," and, therefore, the gilded board with two tenons are firmly fixed in the sockets of silver.

> The Church's one foundation
> Is Jesus Christ her Lord;
> She is His new creation
> By water and the Word;
>
> From heaven He came and sought her,
> To be His holy bride;
> With His own blood he bought her,
> And for her life He died.
>
> Elect from every nation
> Yet one o'er all the earth,
> Her charter of salvation
> One Lord, one faith, one birth;
>
> One holy name she blesses,
> Partakes one holy food,
> And to one hope she presses,
> With every grace endued.

"In him dwelleth all the fulness of the Godhead bodily" (Col. 2: 9). Human wisdom will never be able to understand this, the mystery of the holy Incarnation. Let us worship with the shepherds at that lowly manger in the stable at Bethlehem the babe conceived of the Holy Ghost, born of the virgin Mary.

The boards of the tabernacle, acacia wood, overlaid with gold, speak to us of the twofold nature of our

Lord, the human and divine. The acacia wood speaks of His humanity, the gold of His divinity. "The wages of sin is death." If Christ were to be our substitute and bear the penalty of our sins, He must needs have a human nature. Since children are all alike sharers in perishable human nature, He Himself also, in the same way, took on Him a share of it (Heb. 2: 14). May I point out to you that the words "to be sharers" and "to take a share" are two different words in Greek. Christ's manhood was spotless; He became in the *likeness of sinful flesh*, but He was without sin in the flesh—a mediator between God and man. The Son in whom the Father was well pleased, who did Father's will always and sought Father's glory—*perfect man, perfect God.* Friends, He is the only one whom I want to hold my hand when I walk through the valley of the shadow of death.

Death came by sin (Rom. 6: 23), but He never sinned and no guile was found in his mouth. Being truly human, He was capable of death; being perfect and sinless, death had no hold on Him. His was a *voluntary* death: "I lay it down of myself. I have power to lay it down and take it up again." Of His own freewill He died for you and me.

And yet acacia wood too. "We have not a high priest which *cannot be touched* with the feeling of our infirmities." He can feel for you when you have been for years on a sick-bed. He knows how it feels when you have a headache, and even when you should be without a roof over your head. Remember, "the Son of man had not where to lay his head." He could be weary and hungry; He could weep at the grave of His friend

Lazarus, and rejoice with the young couple at the wedding of Cana. He can be touched; does that not bring Him very near to you?

In the world but not of the world. The leper might touch Him; it would not harm Him. There are worse things than leprosy. Christ came from heaven, the only sinless man that ever walked the earth. He was surrounded by sinful men. His public life was lived in a polluted atmosphere: the hypocrisy of scribes and Pharisees; misunderstood by those who were near Him. He could only feel pity and give love—never wanting to receive, always willing to give. The polluted atmosphere in which He needs had to live could not affect Him. The impurity around Him did not stain His white garment.

"He shall grow up before him as a tender plant, and as a *root out of a dry ground*" (Isa. 53: 2). Acacia wood taken from the desert. Our Lord could find no nourishment in His surroundings, no help—dry ground for the root. "Is not this the son of the carpenter?" His own townspeople asked. Even His brothers believed not on Him. It was to His own disciples, not to scribes and Pharisees, that He addressed those words, full of reproach and grief as He came down from the mount of transfiguration: "O *faithless generation*, how long shall I be with you?" Unbelief in His disciples to whom He had given power to drive out demons. Christ obtained no help from His surroundings, yet that tender plant flourished. What is the secret? He received His life from above; He lived through the Father. That heavenly life He again communicated to His surroundings. I have often seen fir-trees growing on bare rocks. Where do they get their nourishment? How is it possible for a tree to grow on a rock? Botany teaches that those fir-trees have a juice in their roots which penetrates the rock to make room for the rootlets. They give before they take, and this makes it possible for them to flourish, where it would be impossible for other trees to grow—a hidden sacrifice.

Christ's life was a life of constant giving. When He gave His supreme gift on the cross, "when thou shalt make his soul an offering for sin, he *shall see his seed,* he shall prolong his days and the pleasure of the Lord shall prosper in his hand." No fruit without giving, without hidden sacrifices is the law of the kingdom.

How many of God's children complain about their surroundings, their churches—a root in dry ground. For those who "follow the lamb whithersoever he goeth" (Rev. 14: 4), to whom the lamb could give a lamb-like nature, there are no conditions in which they cannot grow. There are two classes of Christians: Getters and Givers. Those who follow the Lamb are givers, and as long as you give you shall *"bring forth fruit* in old age; they shall be fat and flourishing; to shew that the Lord is upright: he is my rock, and there is no unrighteousness in him" (Ps. 92: 14, 15).

Gamblers put in little, and hope to receive a fortune. Let us learn from the Lamb. His motto was: "The Son of man came not to be ministered unto, but to minister, and to give his life a ransom for many" (Matt. 20: 28). Christ sowed first before he reaped.

My dear reader, what are you giving to the circle in which the Lord placed you? Do you bring hidden sacrifices which are so great in the eyes of our heavenly Father? Christ tells us we must lose our life in order to gain it. Christ was a *root in dry ground*, but He redeemed a lost world.

> O Jesus Christ, grow Thou in me
> And all things else recede;
> My heart be daily nearer Thee,
> From sin be daily freed.
>
> Make this poor self grow less and less,
> Be Thou my life and aim;
> Oh, make me daily through Thy grace
> More meet to bear Thy name.

12

SILVER SOCKETS KEEPING THE BOARDS FROM FALLING

19. Thou shalt make forty sockets of silver under the twenty boards.—EXODUS 26: 19

WE have seen in a previous chapter that the tabernacle is a symbol of Christ and also of His Church. We cannot separate the head from the body. A board of acacia wood overlaid with gold is a type of Christ in His twofold nature. Before we meditate on the framework of the tabernacle as a symbol of the Church of Christ and its individual members, I want to draw your attention to the solid foundation of the tabernacle.

Each board of the frame rested with its two tenets in two sockets of silver. This was absolutely necessary. If the two tenets had not been sunk deeply into the socket, the board would never have been able to stand; it would have fallen. These were dovetailed together, and Josephus says that all the sockets closely put together made the impression as if they were one solid foundation of silver. Each of the sockets weighed about an hundredweight and represented the value of about three hundred pounds.

This money was the redemption money which every Israelite over twenty years had to pay as ransom for his soul—no difference was made between rich and poor.

Before God all men are sinners (Rom. 3: 23) and had to be ransomed. No one could enter the army if he had not paid his ransom, which was the same amount for all—half a shekel.

Six hundred and three thousand five hundred and fifty Israelites paid half a shekel; the whole amount came to an hundred talents and 1,775 shekels, so that each of the sockets cost a talent and, therefore, each board needed the ransom of 12,000 men. "Ye know that ye were not redeemed with corruptible things, as silver and gold, but with the precious blood of Christ, as a lamb without blemish and without spot" (1 Pet. 1: 18, 19).

Every Israelite had to pay the ransom money himself. The two tenons connected it with the silver foundation and separated it from the sand of the desert. It is through faith that we accept the Saviour as our sin-bearer. Faith is a personal matter. The mother cannot believe for the daughter nor the father for his son. You can neither eat nor drink for anybody else. Our Lord says: "He that *eateth* my flesh, and *drinketh* my blood, dwelleth in me, and I in him" (John 6: 56).

Desert sand is no suitable foundation for the tabernacle of God and, therefore, the Lord Himself laid the foundation in Zion—a *stone*, a *tried* stone, a precious corner stone, a sure foundation; he *that believeth* does not flee.

Silver socket! You speak to the heart of the believer of the keeping power of our Lord. We could not save ourselves—we discovered that. We cannot sanctify ourselves either. We learned that gradually. Have we learned that we cannot keep ourselves either? Board of acacia wood, listen! Apart from the silver socket you are nothing. You cannot keep yourself either. God never intends us to do what He has reserved for Himself. Oh, for our fruitless efforts! The Holy Spirit will sanctify you; the Lord Jesus will keep you. He is able to keep that which you commit unto Him, the deposit which you commit to His care (2 Tim. 1: 12). Put the keeping of your life into the hands of your Saviour. He is such a faithful, such a reliable guide. He will be true to His trust. You never will be sorry, acacia tree, for having your two tenets in the silver socket.

He is able to keep. However, He can only be responsible for what you commit to His keeping. You have some valuable pictures, and you are going abroad. You feel they might be stolen during your absence, so you bring them to the bank. They are in safe keeping there. You can sleep peacefully and prepare for your voyage. But what about your silver, your table-service? You have had it for so many years now. They were wedding presents from dear friends. Shall you leave them in the house? Shall you ask the manager of your bank to look occasionally in the house to see if all valuables are still there? You are conscious that he would decline such responsibility. He can only be responsible for what you put into his safe keeping. If you commit only a part of your possessions, he will be responsible for a part only. Many of God's children commit only part to the keeping of the Lord. I do not wonder that they often feel anxious and troubled. Commit all to your Lord and keep nothing back. It may perhaps seem a venture of faith to you at first. If you put the direction of your life in His hands, you may wonder where He may lead you. Do you think you can trust Him? Those who trust Him fully will find Him wholly true. Experience will show that all is perfectly safe with Him. His bank is in heaven where neither rust nor moth corrupt, where thieves do not break in and steal. The more you entrust to Him, the better you will know Him. The result will be a perfect confidence in your keeper. You will be able to say: "I know whom I have believed, and am persuaded that he is able to keep that which I have committed unto him against that day" (2 Tim. 1: 12). The joybells will begin to ring in your heart, for I feel sure real joy, joy of the Holy Ghost, will come only when all is committed, all is deposited in the pierced hands of your risen Saviour.

"He is able to *keep you from falling*, and to present you faultless before the presence of his glory *with exceeding joy*" (Jude, verse 24). Thanks be unto God for His unspeakable gift; thanks be to Him for the silver socket for the board of acacia wood.

Board of acacia wood, you need not be afraid that the silver socket weighing a hundredweight will not be able to hold you. Let your whole weight full on it, so that you get as near as possible to the silver. A lady missionary to India had been visiting with her native Bible woman one day—one Zenana after the other. Everywhere she had to answer numberless questions. She was not yet used to the climate and felt very weary. She could hardly continue her Bible-reading. The native sister noticed it, and taking a seat behind the missionary, asked the missionary to lean against her. The sister hardly liked to let her whole weight rest on the slender native woman. "If you really love me, you must lean hard." Dear reader, have you some heavy burden now to bear? Perhaps you are praying for the salvation of one of your dear ones and the answer does not seem to come; your husband is unemployed; your business goes back; your health is failing; listen to the voice of your Saviour who loved you enough to die for you. Listen, what He says to you: "If you love me, lean hard."

LEAN HARD

Child of my love, "lean hard,"
And let me feel the pressure of thy care.
I know thy burden, child; I shaped it,
Poised in Mine own hand, made no proportion
In its weight to thine unaided strength;
For ever as I laid it on I said,—
"I shall be near, *and while she leans on Me,*
This burden shall be Mine, not hers;
So shall I keep My child within the circling arms
Of Mine own love." *Here lay it down,* nor fear
To impose it on a Shoulder which upholds
The government of worlds. *Yet closer* come,
Thou are not near enough; I would embrace thy care.
So I might *feel* My child reposing on My breast.
Thou lovest Me? I know it. Doubt not, then,
But, loving Me, lean hard.

—Selected

13

THE HOLY SPIRIT AND THE WOOD OF THE ACACIA TREE

15. And thou shalt make boards for the tabernacle of acacia wood standing up.
29. And thou shalt *overlay* the *boards* with gold, and make their rings (staples) of gold for places for the bars: and thou shalt overlay the *bars with gold.*
—Exodus 26: 15, 29

Forty boards of acacia wood, eighteen feet high, two feet nine inches in breadth, formed the framework of the tabernacle. The acacia tree was one of the trees found in the desert. It was the proletariat amongst the desert trees. God's choice differs from ours. "God hath chosen the foolish things of the world to confound the wise, . . . yea, and things *which are not,* to bring to nought things that are: that no flesh should glory in his presence" (1 Cor. 1: 27–29). If we want to make a good piece of work, we require good material from which to make it. The Holy Spirit can make the most wonderful piece of art in the world: a poor sinner transformed into the image of the Master, out of very poor material. He can transform a Jacob into Israel. He can make use of the acacia tree in the desert to make the framework of the tabernacle, His Church on earth, members of the body of Christ.

Of course, all the forty boards were not taken from one tree. Most probably each tree furnished only one board. Neither were they all hewn down at the same time or at the same place. At the different halting-places they looked out for suitable trees. There is a great variety among the members of the body. It is "a *multitude,* which no man can number, of all nations, and kindreds, and people and tongues" (Rev. 7: 9). Men, women, and children too (praise the Lord); some rich, many poor, simple folks, like the majority of us, but also some of the highest culture, men prominent in science and art; for it is a great mistake to assume that all men of science are unbelievers—God has His chosen ones amongst all nations and in all classes of society.

Different in many ways, yet all alike sprang from native soil and had to be taken out of the desert before they could take their place in the framework of the tabernacle: brought out of darkness into His marvellous light. The Word of our Lord applied to all and each one: "Except ye be *born again,* ye cannot see the kingdom of God. Except a man be born of water and of the Spirit, he cannot *enter* into the kingdom of God" (John 3: 3, 5).

In another way, too, they were all alike. Each board with its two tenets had to rest in the silver socket. "The church's one foundation is Jesus Christ her Lord." "Other foundation can no man lay than that is laid, which is Jesus Christ" (1 Cor. 3: 11).

Very different, too, were the ways by which the different boards found their way into the framework of the tabernacle. The Holy Spirit has different ways to bring us to Christ. Many find the Lord in their youth, the best and easiest time to make a decision for Christ. The older one gets, the more difficult it may become, but praise the Lord, old people can be saved too. Some are brought to Christ by a deep conviction of sin; to others the heinousness, the awful character of sin becomes clear after their conversion. Some know the exact day and hour of their conversion, others do not. Each board has its own story to tell.

I love testimony meetings. I rejoice to hear that something is happening. It does my heart good when I listen to bright testimonies, especially from young Christians. I am sure they may be a powerful inducement for others to decide for Christ. I wonder why they are not so frequent as they used to be. May it be that they are happening less? I propose to hold a testimony meeting now and ask one of the boards of acacia wood to tell its story.

"At one time," he says, "I was an acacia tree in the desert. I grew out of it. All my nourishment I got from the earth. God had cursed the earth. As long as I was rooted in the desert I could not possibly have a place in the tabernacle. I had necessarily to be taken out of the desert soil, from which I drew all my nourishment.

"One day a stranger came, his name was Bezaleel. He looked at me and at the other trees near me. Then he came back and smiled. With his knife he made a mark on me. I was the only one in the grove he marked. At the time I did not know what it meant. Afterward I found out he had chosen me for a board in the tabernacle. Why he chose me and not the others I really cannot tell. I feel sure I was not any better than the others."

The ministry of the Holy Spirit has not the aim of converting the world. The world will never be converted. Our Lord said that instead of getting better, it would grow worse. The Holy Spirit is gathering out of all nations, those whom God the Father of our Lord Jesus Christ has *chosen* in Him before the foundation of the world (Eph. 1: 4), "*elect* according to the fore-knowledge of God the Father, through sanctification of the Spirit" (1 Pet. 1: 2). The Greek word for church is "Ecclesia," the called-out one. Every child of God is a living proof for the ministry of the Holy Spirit. We beg the board's pardon for interrupting him. He continues, however:

"Then I must have been a called-out one," he says, "for there were other trees quite as high and strong as I, but the Master chose me. I can never thank Him enough for that. But then came a day I shall never forget. A man came with a strong axe and put it to my roots. Blow after blow fell. At last I fell and died. I had to be separated entirely from the desert life. That was necessary.

"Do not think I was ready now for a board in the tabernacle. God took a great deal of pains with me. Do you remember what God said about Ephraim? 'Therefore have I hewed them by the prophets; I have slain them by the words of my mouth' (Hosea 6: 5). He did the same with me. I had to be planed. That was necessary again. I should not have fitted into my place otherwise. I did not always like it. Sometimes I blamed the prophets. I thought somebody had told them some of my secrets. I became angry with them and I forgot that they did their planning at the bidding of their Lord. It had to be, for there was so much of my old nature which would never have fitted in the tabernacle, rough corners which had to be planed away. Sometimes the Master Himself took the plane in His hand. I did not mind that. He always gave me a kind word and filled my heart with hope when He told me of coming glory and what He was going to make from me. It seemed to me He was like the silversmith sitting near the fire, awaiting the moment that His face was reflected in the silver" (Mal. 3: 3).

I am sure you have been listening with interest to the testimony of our board. So have I, for my experience has been somewhat similar and I beg his forgiveness when I interrupt him once more.

The board was right when it said that God had taken great trouble with him; so He has with me. The Holy Spirit longs to transform us in the glorious image of our Lord (2 Cor. 3: 18). He wants to make us Christlike. Christ in us is the hope of glory, the way to become glorious.

The Holy Spirit employs different means to achieve His purpose. He brings us together with other people or in other surroundings and it seems as if we are turned inside out. We discover hidden failures in our innermost heart which are never suspected to be there. In Egypt the children of Israel found out that the Egyptians were hard taskmasters. In the desert they found out what they themselves were. If Moses had told them in Egypt that the time would come that they would murmur against Jehovah who had led them out of the house of bondage, they would have answered, "Impossible." When they were led into the desert and no longer could sit by the fleshpots of Egypt, six hundred thousand men failed in the testing and only two men, Joshua and Caleb, passed their examination and profited by God's dealings with them (Num. 14: 24).

The Lord may use worldly people, unholy people, and put the plane in their hands. Jacob was certainly selfish; it may be that he himself was not fully conscious of it. Esau had reason to know it. God wanted to transform Jacob into an Israel. He sent him to Laban. Laban was even more selfish than Jacob. God showed Jacob what selfishness was. I can imagine Jacob coming home to his Rachel in the evening when Laban had been especially trying and saying, "Rachel, dear, I do not want to hurt you, but your father is the most selfish man I ever met—how I hate selfishness." God wanted to make out of Jacob an Israel, a prince of God, an over-comer. He was training Jacob all that time with Laban. When Jacob had learned his lesson, God allowed him to return and at Peniel to become a new man with a new name.

Peninnah had children; Hannah had none. Some women can be mean, and Peninnah was. She made Hannah's life hard. Hannah shed many a tear but she did not say, "I cannot stand this life any longer, I must run away. I shall get a divorce." No, she let Peninnah become a blessing to her. She took her trouble to God and God gave her a Samuel. She had passed her test. Do you think Hannah could ever have sung that choice idyll, as simple as beautiful, reminding us in its prophetic character of the Magnificat of the virgin, if she had not been trained in the hard school of Peninnah?

It may be that some of my readers are in the school of Laban or Peninnah. Remember, it is God who brought you together with your Laban. He intends you for a board in the tabernacle. Your Laban is one of the *"all things"* which all work together, each one of them to your supreme good, to become like unto your Lord (Rom. 8 : 28). Your Father takes so much pains with your training because He wants to make something special out of you. If you feel tempted to be cross at your Laban say: "Laban, you are one of the 'all things.' You are planing me that I may become a board of acacia overlaid with gold."

May I ask you a question? *Have you ever prayed* for your Laban? If you do this in harmony with the Spirit, you will begin to love him. One other question. Have you *ever really thanked God* for your Laban? Do you know that you ought to? "Giving thanks *always* for *all things* unto God and the Father in the name of our Lord Jesus Christ." *"Always* for *all things"* (Eph. 5 : 20).

Let us listen once more to our board; it does not mind my interruptions. "You want to know what happened to me then? The Master did put me again in the desert, but this time it was all different. It had all become new. In fact, I have become a new creature. Something has happened inside of me and outside as well. I do not belong any more to the desert. If you look at me, you will see that I am standing in two silver sockets. I like to call them grace and truth. The sockets stand between me and the desert. I am in the world, but not of the world (John 17 : 14). The whole direction of my life has been changed. I have other aims for my life now. Formerly the blackbirds of the air made their nest in me; now I have been transplanted from darkness into light. I stand on quite a different foundation. I am a board in the house of God. I cannot tell you how happy I am now. I need not fear the typhoon of the desert any more. I am rooted and grounded in my Lord. I am not alone any more. There are other boards on either side of me, and we are so closely united together that we form together one solid wall—all one in Christ Jesus." And after a pause— "Look at me, you see that I am different. Do you know me still? You cannot see my wood at all. I am *overlaid with gold*. 'I am crucified with Christ: nevertheless I live; yet not I, but *Christ liveth in me*: and the life which I now live in the flesh *I live by faith of the Son of God*, who loved me, and gave himself for me'" (Gal. 2: 20).

A board of acacia wood from the desert and now a place in the framework of the tabernacle. Is this possible? Certainly not, if God had not said: "Thou *shalt overlay them with gold*" (Exod. 26: 29). Nothing more is to be seen of the acacia wood; and if the tenons were not covered with gold, they were hidden in the socket of silver.

Can this transformation become a reality in the life of God's children? When the apostle says, "For ye are dead, and your life is hid with Christ in God" (Col. 3: 3), does he really mean it? Is this experience possible in the life of every child of God?

To answer this question, in fault of better words, I want to employ the words *State* and *Standing*. For many years an English solicitor had been looking for the sole heir of one of the oldest noble families. At last he was successful in discovering him as a poor colonist in Australia. The man was poor, living in wretched circumstances, in winter often being in great need. This was his *state*. His *standing* was the heir of a nobleman, having millions at his disposal. For many years he was in complete ignorance of his standing. As soon as he was informed of his good fortune, his state became, of course, also different.

Our standing has to do with our *justification,* our state with our sanctification, though naturally it is not possible to separate justification and sanctification completely from each other.

Paul in the Epistles often makes use of the expression, "In Christ." Sometimes it refers to our state, sometimes to our standing When he writes, "There is therefore now *no condemnation* to them which are *in Christ Jesus*," (Rom. 8: 1), he refers to our *standing*. Our state shows what use we make of our standing, how far we let it become a reality in our lives.

Let us first meditate on our state. To be in Christ, as far as our justification is concerned, the standing of man is either "in Christ" or "in Adam." The unrenewed man is *"in Adam."* Humanity is not a sand-heap in which every grain of sand is alive, but a living organism, a tree consisting of thousands of particles which are, however, all connected. In Adam the whole human race was tested. There was only one testing and Adam failed in it and we in him. It is important that we realize we are lost!

To such lost people the gospel comes. The good news is not that God once more offers us another test. When a tree is cut down with its roots, it is dead. The only way is to graft a branch on a new root. "Therefore if any man be *in Christ,* he is a *new creature*" (2 Cor. 5: 17). He gets a new *standing*. He is no longer in

Adam, but *in Christ.* It is not a gradual process; it does not mean gradually to grow out of Adam into Christ. It is a definite transplanting done in a definite moment; out of Adam into Christ. You have a new standing. We learned a chorus:

> And the end is not yet, praise the Lord!
> Blessings new He is bestowing
> And my cup is overflowing
> And the end is not yet, praise the Lord!

We have not exhausted the meaning of to be "in Christ" when at the new birth our *standing* has become "in Christ."

Our *walk* should also be in Christ. How happy a child is when it is conscious that Father is pleased with him. It is just the same with the relation between us and Christ. When we are conscious that there is nothing between Christ and us that interrupts communion with Him, that His power can flow through us, and that we can do all things through Christ, who strengthens us (Phil. 4: 13), then our walk is also in Christ; that we are "in Christ" not only for our justification, but also for our sanctification.

When your walk is in Christ, He can communicate His life to you. His life was a life of obedience. He never turned back (Isa. 50: 5). He came to do His Father's will. When your life is hidden in Christ, when the board of acacia wood is overlaid with gold, you will also be in harmony with the will of Father. Whatever Father bids you do, your response will also be "I delight to do thy will." Christ was obedient until death. When your walk is in Christ, you have been crucified with Him. You cannot make the Christ-life in you fuller and more active than it is. You need not do it either. In Him is the fullness of the Godhead bodily, but you can every day and every hour reckon your own life, with its wishes and plans, dead. After having done this, this should be your constant walk. The more your own life is given to die, the more His life will become powerful in you, and His resurrection life and power will be manifested to you. Acacia wood, you are overlaid with fine gold!

Do I not need the Lord's power any more now? I need Him more than ever. The power is not in me, but in Him. He is the power-house. Only as long as I abide in Him can His power flow through me. In our Lord we find all we need, but you only get it if you are in touch with Him. You can never be independent of Him. In times past when there was neither gas nor electricity in a country house, a number of candlesticks were placed in the hall. You could light one candle from the other and then you needed it no more. The relation between Christ and us is different. The train does not move until it is connected with the engine. "Abide in me, and I in you. As the branch cannot bear fruit of itself, except it abide in the vine; no more can ye, except ye abide in me. I am the vine, ye are the branches: He that abideth in me, and I in him, the same bringeth forth much fruit: for *without* me (apart from me) ye can do *nothing*" (John 15: 4–5).

In the prayer of intercession which our Lord may have prayed in Gethsemane He prayed: "Neither pray I for these alone, but for them also which shall believe on me through their word; that *they all may be one*" (John 17: 20–21). "Behold, how good and how pleasant it is for brethren to *dwell together in unity*! For there *commanded the Lord blessing*, even life for ever more" (Ps. 133: 1, 3). "All one in Christ Jesus"—the bond that unites the members of the one body of Christ is far closer, far more precious than that which unites us with unconverted relatives or with our fellow countrymen. This alliance is not made by man, neither need be made with men. It was made on the cross of Golgotha.

Five bars of acacia wood overlaid with gold, fastened in staples of gold, held the twenty boards on each side closely and firmly together. The two at the top and at the foot came half way and met in the middle; the middle bar reached from end to end. These bars together with the silver sockets helped to bear the boards up and keep them from falling down.

I. The lowest bar joining God's children together reminds us that God's children all over the world have all the word of God as food for their souls. There is far more that unites God's children than what separates them. Where the heart is full of Jesus, where He is the subject of our conversations, we come close together. It has been my privilege many years to come to the Conference at Keswick. More than five thousand of God's children meet there from many countries, all with the longing desire to come closer to the Lord. Speakers and hearers come from many denominations, but the question is not asked: to which denomination do you belong? The Keswick motto is: "All one in Christ Jesus."

II. The second bar tells us that *united prayer* joins God's children together. I thank the Lord for the week of universal prayer. What rivers of blessing have issued from those meetings at the beginning of the year; when you have been together on your knees you cannot very well get up to combat each other.

III. The third bar tells us that there is one bread we break, one table spread for us. I have been told that when General Washington with his army was encamped before Morristown, he heard that the next Sunday there was Holy Communion in the village church. He paid a visit to the pastor and said to him, "You are a Presbyterian; I do not know whether your church allows Christians from other churches to join you in the holy meal." The pastor gave the excellent answer, "General, the table is not the table of the Presbyterians, but the Lord's table." May the Lord's Supper, which should bind all members of His body together, never be the cause of separation amongst them.

IV. The next bar tells us there is still another bond that joins God's children together. "And above all these things *put on love*, which is the *bond of perfectness*. And let the peace of God rule in your hearts, to the which also ye are called in one body" (Col. 3: 14–15). The more Christ is formed in us, the more we approach and love the brethren. The opposite holds also: if we are standing in a circle and our blessed Lord is in the midst, the nearer we get to each other, the nearer we get to Him. When two mountaineers climb a mountain from opposite sides, the higher they ascend, the nearer they get to each other. When both have reached the summit they are together.

V. The fifth bar joins the boards from the inside and goes through the midst of the wood. When one goes to different churches one often hears the complaint that there is so little brotherly love. We need not be surprised at it; the middle bar is lacking. If we want more love, we must be filled with the Holy Ghost. That is the bond that unites us closer together. The love of God is poured out in our hearts through the Holy Ghost (Rom. 5:5). Where the Holy Spirit presides there is unity amongst God's children.

Happy board of acacia wood, overlaid with gold. Blessed is the day when Bezaleel marked you, the day when you were cut down and planed to fill a place in the tabernacle of God.

Acacia wood overlaid with gold. I trust Dr. Ironside will forgive me if I tell a story he told us fifteen years ago at a Bible conference at Ocean City. A friend of his, a medical missionary in Central Africa, was one day visiting some outlying stations. As he was riding through the woods, his horse became restless and pricked up its ears. He heard groaning and sobbing. He dismounted, bound his horse to a tree and began to search the woods. He found a young woman covered with sores and ulcers. Her relatives had laid her there in the woods to die. The doctor fetched fresh water and began to wash the ulcers and alleviate her pains. He tore his shirt in strips and bound her wounds. Then he took her tenderly in his arms and held her on his horse as he trudged by her side the ten miles to his hospital. The nurses put her in a bath, washed the wounds, and put her in a soft, clean bed. All prayed that the Lord might do a miracle and spare that young life. The Lord heard their prayers and gradually she recovered and regained her strength. But they wanted more. They wanted her soul to be healed, and told her the glad news of a Saviour who had come from heaven to die for her. They prayed that she might go back to her native village with the love of the Saviour in her heart. He loved her so much, they urged her to love Him too. At that moment the doctor opened the door and just looked in. Her whole face lit up, "Nurse, is He like my doctor? Then I'll love Him too. Is he like my doctor?" I think that medical missionary was an acacia tree overlaid with gold.

THE HIS POEM (Eph. 2: 10)

"Then saw I how, before a master wise
    A shapeless stone was set;
He said, 'Therein a form of beauty lies,
    Though none behold it yet.'

"When all beside it shall be hewn away
    That glorious shape shall stand
In beauty of the everlasting day
    Of the unsullied land!

"When hewn and shaped till self no more is found,
    Self ended at the cross;
The precious freed from all the vile around,
    No gain, but blessed loss.

"Thus Christ alone remains—the former things
    Forever passed away,
And unto Him the heart in gladness sings
    All through the weary day."

—H. Suso

14

THE CURTAINS AND COVERINGS
OF THE TABERNACLE

And thou shalt make a covering for the tent of
rams' skins dyed red, and a covering above of
badgers' skins.—EXODUS 26: 14

WE have been meditating on the boards overlaid with
gold sunk deep into the sockets of silver. The bars
taught us that each one of us, though we have to come
personally to the Saviour as individuals, are also closely
united together: one faith, one hope, one baptism, one
throne of grace where our prayers meet, one bread we
break, one bond of perfection, the bond of love. The
middle bar, although hidden from our eyes, teaches us:
We have one Holy Spirit who sanctifies us, who reminds
us of our Lord, who teaches us all truth, and gives us
the power to become fruit-bearing branches of the vine.

On this foundation a roof of curtains and covering
is resting. God's children have a roof over their houses
although the Master Himself often had not where to
lay His head (Matt. 8: 20). The roof of the tabernacle
consisted of four different coverings: fine twined linen,
of goats' hair, of rams' skins, and an outside covering
of badgers' skins. With willing hearts the men had
brought them as an offering to the Lord (Exod. 25: 4–5).
The women did not want to be left behind. They gave
their time and their skill. Women *whose hearts* had

Curtains and Coverings of the Holy Place

been stirred spun goats' hair. *Wise-hearted* women spun with their hands and brought that which they had spun: blue, purple, scarlet, and fine linen (Exod. 35: 25–26). It was no easy work; the stitching was hard. Their hands, like St. Paul's when making tents and sails, must often have hurt them, but where love has stirred the hearts, no task is difficult. A busy scene in which our Father in heaven must have been delighted.

The covering which could be seen from the inside was of fine linen embroidered blue, purple and scarlet. There were ten curtains each fourteen yards long and two yards wide; five curtains were joined together for one large curtain, and the two were joined together by fifty loops which were joined by fifty golden clasps. They were joined over the vail which separated the Holy of holies from the sanctuary. The one curtain covered the sanctuary; the second, the Holy of holies on the west side of the tabernacle.

This beautiful inner curtain was covered by one of goats' hair. You will notice that each curtain was one yard longer than the curtain it covered. The linen curtain did not quite reach to the ground, but the one of goats' hair covered all three sides, and the extra length was folded double and hung over the outer vail at the east end. A third covering was of rams' skins dyed red, and above this was a covering of badgers' skins.

It has been suggested by some students that the tabernacle had a sloping roof to prevent the rain from falling into the sanctuary. I cannot agree with this. God gives us the most minute description of the construction of the tabernacle. I find no mention whatever of the pole on which the curtains had to rest and how this pole had to be fixed. I take it that the skins were impervious to rain, and when these skins were stretched over the boards so as to provide a flat surface, hardly any rain would remain on the roof, and this in the hot climate would quickly evaporate.

I am sure it will be clear to every reader that the roof on the tabernacle points to our blessed Lord. Jesus is our roof. We are living in ominous times, the child of God is safe under this roof. Have you ever meditated on the 57th Psalm? Is your heart troubled? Are you wondering what the future holds in store for you? Look up at that beautiful roof of white, blue, scarlet and purple. Look at the cherubim. They give glory to the blessed Trinity. Cry unto the most High. His ears are always open to the cry of His people. He will perform all things for you and in you. His twin-angels, mercy and truth, will be your companions even in a lion's den. Be merciful unto me, O God; be merciful unto me: for my soul trusteth in thee: yet, in *the shadow of thy wings* will I make my refuge (Ps. 57: 1). Christ is the head in whom all the building is fitly framed together (Eph. 2: 20–21). There should be no empty space between the boards and the roof. Chrysostrom knew this when he said, "Nothing should come between head and body; they are closely united together."

Each of the four curtains, as the four Gospels, presents a different aspect of our Saviour. His personality is too manifold to be fully represented by one type. "In him dwelleth *all the fulness of the Godhead* bodily" (Col. 2: 9).

A covering of badgers' skins. Commentators differ somewhat in their opinion about the material of the outer covering and what is exactly to be understood by it. The Septuagint translates the Hebrew word "Achah" by "skins of blue leather." Shoes were made out of it (Ezek. 16: 10). A Moabite looking down from his hills on the tabernacle would fail to understand why the Israelites thought so much of it. To him it looked like a large black coffin. He knew nothing about the splendour of its interior. He saw only the badgers' skins.

Is it not the same today? The world considers Christ's teaching impractical. Christ tells His disciples to "seek first the kingdom of God and His righteousness; and all other things shall be added unto you" (Matt. 6: 33). The world says, "Push your way to the front by whatever means you can." The weak have to go to the wall. You must have room to live for yourself, for might is right. No, the present world stage has no room for a Christ who was willing to give His life on the cross to save His enemies. If His principles were to prevail, it would upset all their plans, but looking around them they feel sure they do not and never will. They do not think about Christ; they are indifferent to Him; they see no beauty in Him. They see only the badgers' skins.

That badgers' skin speaks to us of a Saviour who emptied Himself of His glory and took the form of a servant (Phil. 2: 7), of One who had come "not to be ministered unto, but to minister, to give His life a ransom for many" (Matt. 20: 28). It speaks of a high priest, who on the day of atonement put aside His garment of glory and put on the linen coat (Lev. 16: 4). It speaks of the Son of man, who less than foxes and birds, had not where to lay His head (Luke 9: 58).

Need we wonder that His gospel was to the Greeks

foolishness and to the Jews a stumbling-block? (1 Cor. 1: 23). They were expecting a Messiah who would deliver them out of the hands of the Romans; they wanted the curtain of white linen, of blue, purple and scarlet, and forgot that the curtain of badgers' skins had to come first. He had no form nor comeliness for them; and when they saw Him, they saw no beauty that they should desire Him (Isa. 53: 2). One of the most pathetic statements in John's Gospel, one that brings tears in our eyes as I am sure it did in the eyes of the aged disciple, one that made our Saviour weep as He was bearing His cross to Golgotha, is: *"He came into his own, and his own received him not"* (John 1: 11).

Who stands highest, can stoop lowest. "Jesus knowing that the Father had given all things into his hands, and that he was come from God, and went to God; laid aside his garments and took a towel and girded himself, and washed his disciples' feet" (John 13: 3–5). It is the king's son that can do the slave's work. He is not afraid to lose his dignity. The royal motto of the Prince of Wales is: "Ich dien"—"I serve." This too is the best motto for the children of the King. May the Holy Spirit open our eyes to see the beauty of the badgers' skins. May this mind be in us which was also in Christ Jesus (Phil. 2: 5).

The Master went to Gethsemane, to the valley of shadows, with a song on His lips. It is also the way His disciples have to go if their life is to be fruitful and a blessing to others. "If Christ died for all, *we are dead*; and He died for all that they which live should not henceforth live unto themselves but unto him which died for them and rose again" (2 Cor. 5: 14, 15). Not live for ourselves, but for *others*. The corn of wheat has to fall into the ground and die if it is to bring forth much fruit (John 12: 24).

Covering of badgers' skins, teach us again and again that a lack of humility, a protruding of self is the greatest hindrance to a fruitful ministry. The servants the Master can use best are those who have discovered the preciousness of the badgers' skins. You will learn it in the school of Jesus. He says: "Learn of me, for *I am meek and lowly in heart*" (Matt. 11: 29).

A covering for the tent of rams' skins dyed red was beneath the covering of badgers' skins. The ram was a *clean* animal. At the consecration of the priests two rams were offered. The one was a burnt-offering, the other for consecration. Of its blood, Moses put upon the tip of the right ear, the thumb of the right hand, and upon the great toe of Aaron's sons at their consecration (Lev. 8: 24). Holy Spirit, remind me of the blood on my right ear, when it was bored as I gave myself to the service of my Lord, as I knelt in the sanctuary and praying hands were laid on my head at my ordination fifty years ago. Holy Spirit, open my ears to listen to Thy voice, teaching me and sending me on Thy errands, and may the blood on my ear close it to the insinuations of Satan. May the blood on my thumb direct me in my writing, and the blood on my toe keep my feet from going anywhere whither I am not sent by Thee! "Blessed is the man that heareth me, watching daily at my gates, waiting at the posts of my doors" (Prov. 8: 34).

The covering of rams' skins dyed red points us to our Saviour, who came not only to serve, but to *suffer*. "Though he were a Son, yet learned he obedience by the things which he suffered" (Heb. 5: 8). He came to suffer, to suffer for you, for me. You may remember the picture of the young child helping His father in the carpenter's shop. As the young boy stretched out His arms, the mother, watching, saw the shadow of the cross. The artist was right. All through life the cross threw its dark shadow before Him. He knew about the cruel mocking and scourging, Gethsemane and Golgotha. And yet He could say: "The Lord God hath opened mine ear, and *I was not rebellious*, neither turned away my back. *I gave my back to the smiters*, and my cheek to them that plucked off the hair: I hid not my face *from shame and spitting*" (Isa. 50: 5, 6).

Many a time in His thoughts He must have seen the dark cypresses of Gethsemane, the rugged cross at the end of the journey. He knew it all, and yet when the time was come, *He steadfastly set His face to go to Jerusalem.*

Do you wish to gauge some little of the meaning of those rams' skins dyed red? Go with me to Morijah. Do you see that old man wearily making his way to the summit? Do you see that lad at his side full of life and vigour? God's precious gift after twenty-five long years of praying and waiting? Listen to his question: "My father."

And he said: "Here am I, my son."

"Behold the fire and the wood: but where is a lamb for a burnt-offering?"

"God will provide, laddie."

I do not think many words were spoken between these two. Watch those two when they stood near the altar, those two who were bound together in such close love. What they said to each other no human ear ever heard.

"Child, can you trust me and love me still, even when you do not understand me? God has spoken to me. He told me to take you, my only one, my beloved one." His voice became halting and soft. "He—told me to offer you!" Do you see how those two in silence embrace each other and how the lad laid himself on the altar?

"Father, you need not bind me. I shall lay quietly and not move." Do you see that outstretched hand with the knife ready to slay?

Listen, there is a voice from heaven: "Lay not thine hand upon the lad—now I know that thou fearest God, seeing thou hast not withheld thy son, thine only son from me" (Gen. 22: 15, 16).

Abraham's son was spared, but God did not spare His own Son, but delivered Him up for us all (Rom. 8: 32). That is the rams' skins dyed red.

Rams' skins dyed red! Here we shall never fully understand thy meaning; we shall know hereafter. You point us to that lonely one in the garden kneeling down and whose sweat was as it were *great drops of blood* falling down to the ground. Not even an hour His disciples could watch with Him. He trod the wine-press alone. "Father, if thou be willing, remove this cup from me: nevertheless not my will, but thine be done" (Luke 22: 42).

Rams' skins dyed red, you tell me what it cost my Saviour to redeem me, to bring me out of darkness into His marvellous light. "Redeemed not by corruptible things, as silver and gold, but with the precious blood of Christ, as of a lamb without blemish and without spot" (1 Pet. 1: 18, 19). You teach me what unmeasurable value a single soul has for our Lord. He reckoned no price too high to pay to save a soul from destruction. Remind me each time I am brought together with unconverted men and women, that the burden of their souls may be laid on my heart.

Rams' skins dyed red! You humble me, for my sins too have given thee that red colour. I feel ashamed that even after my conversion, through my fault, thou hast been drenched with blood. What are those wounds in Thy hands? "Those with which I was wounded in the *house of my friends*" (Zech. 13: 6). Master, I know such wounds hurt most. I know such scars take longest to heal. Teach me to hate sin as Thou dost hate it; teach me to love the sinner with Thy seeking love!

15

CURTAINS OF GOATS' HAIR AND FINE TWINED LINEN

7. And thou shalt make curtains of goats' hair to be a covering upon the tabernacle.

9. And thou shalt couple *five* curtains by themselves, and shalt double the *sixth curtain* in the forefront of the tabernacle.—EXODUS 26: 7, 9

THE curtain of goats' hair was near the covering of rams' skins. From the outside it was the third covering; counting from the inside, it was the second covering, the embroidered curtain of fine twined linen. The Holy Spirit draws our special attention to it, giving a detailed description of it. It was different from the other coverings in that there were eleven curtains instead of ten, and that it was one yard longer than the curtains of linen.

The goats we saw in Palestine were small and mostly black. There are, however, some species having fine, white, silky hair, like that of the Angora goat, and I like to think with many commentators that these were chosen for the tabernacle. Nothing can be good enough for the house of God. The eleventh curtain was doubled up in the forefront of the tabernacle; the other curtains could be so arranged that they spanned the roof and hung down and covered the south and north walls as well as the back wall, so that the tabernacle was entirely

**The High Priest of Israel in His Robes
of Glory and Beauty**

covered by the goats' hair skins. It would be possible so to arrange this curtain that a border could be seen at the foot of the cherubim curtains; and if we are right in the assumption that white goats were chosen, their white, silky hair would furnish a beautiful white border.

At every one of the great Jewish feasts, the feast of unleavened bread, the feast of the first fruits, the feast of Ingathering at Pentecost, and the Day of Atonement, the goat had to be the sin-offering. It seems to me, therefore, that the coverings of goats' hair teach us two most important facts of our Christian life.

Substitution and Forgiveness: God instituted the Feast of Passover to be kept on the fourteenth day of the month of Abib. He said: "This month shall be unto you the beginning of months: it shall be the first month of the year to you" (Exod. 12: 2). It shows the importance God attached to the deliverance of His people out of the bondage of Egypt, and He wished His people to consider it in the same light. An old officer met my colleague and told him it was his birthday. My friend asked him how old he was and the answer was, "Seven years today." It was seven years ago that he had given his heart to the Saviour, that he was born again. The old major had two birthdays and considered that the latter was the time he really began to live. Reader, have you also two birthdays?

The feast of unleavened bread (Deut. 16: 3) was closely connected with the Passover. It began on the day after the Passover. No leaven was to be found in their houses and during those seven days, only un-leavened bread was eaten—a custom still kept up by the Jews till this day. Leaven in the Old Testament is always mentioned in an evil sense. It is a symbol of sin and corruption. On every day of this week a goat was offered for a sin-offering.

The feast of the firstfruits (Exod. 23: 19) was celebrated in spring. Young and old were longing to see the first green sprouting out of the earth. It was also connected with the Passover. It is clear that they could only celebrate it after they had left the wilderness behind them, crossed the Jordan, and settled in the land. The firstfruit belonged to the Lord. This was only right. I do not think I ever ate the first strawberries in our garden or the first peach. I kept them for somebody I liked better than myself. It was waved before the Lord for His acceptance. It was followed by the different sacrifices, the sin-offering being a goat.

The Holy Spirit teaches us the meaning of the feast of the firstfruits. It foreshadowed *Christ risen from the dead.* "Christ the firstfruits; afterward they that are Christ's at his coming" (1 Cor. 15: 23). This is comfort when we stand at an open grave: *"I live, ye shall live also"* (John 14: 19).

Seven weeks later on the feast of Pentecost with grateful hearts, the children of Israel brought the Lord a tribute of the first sheaves of corn in joyful expectation of the harvest which was to follow. How the Master's heart rejoices when day by day souls are brought into the fold, both Jews and Gentiles, bringing the day of His coming nearer. Then the great harvest festival will take place when He comes in the clouds for His own.

Those sheaves of corn make our hearts rejoice. They speak of new life, resurrection life. That does not mean, however, that the old nature has been eradicated. Even to the church of the firstborn (Heb. 12: 23) the Lord says: "Take ye a kid of the goats for a sin-offering." "Thanks be unto God for his unspeakable gift"—the curtains of goats' hair (2 Cor. 9: 15).

The day of Atonement (described in Leviticus 16 and 23). Christ our high priest; Christ the sacrifice. How the people looked forward to that day! It was on the tenth day of the seventh month that the high priest offered sacrifices for himself and the people. It was on that day and on that day only that the high priest entered the Holy of holies. May I ask you to read carefully Leviticus 16 and the explanation the Holy Spirit gives us in Hebrews 9. He tells us how the Holiest of holies is the embodiment of the Holiness of God. He tells us how Christ made a new and living way through the vail that is His flesh; and that now the way into the holiest is open for each child of God; and that not only once a year, but that at any time we may come in full assurance to the throne of grace; that it is even possible always to be in the conscious presence of the most High. How sad it is that so many believers remain in the outer court and so miss the joy of the Holy Ghost, for in His presence is fullness of joy, at his right hand pleasures for evermore (Ps. 16: 11).

The high priest in Israel was a sinner as the people. He, therefore, had to sacrifice first a bullock as a sin-offering for himself. Our high priest need not do this. God has made Him to be sin for us *who knew no sin.*

The curtains of goats' hair speak to us of *Substitution* and Forgiveness. Two goats were presented to the

Lord at the door of the tabernacle on the day of atonement. The sacrifice Christ made for us on Golgotha is so many-sided that one symbol would not be sufficient. Lots were cast upon the two goats. The one upon whom the Lord's lot fell was slain as a sin-offering for the people, and the high priest brought its blood within the vail and sprinkled it on the mercy-seat to make an atonement for the *uncleanness* of the *children* of Israel because of *their transgressions* in *all* their sins.

In Christ we have our place in the Holiest. Christ tasted death in all its bitterness for us. The curtains of goats' hair speak of substitution. He entered the holiest through the vail with His own blood. His glorious resurrection was the pledge that God had accepted the sacrifice and now there is no longer a vail between our heavenly Father and His children.

The Lord's goat had been offered as a sin-offering, the blood sprinkled on the mercy-seat. God had taken away everything which could hinder the people from approaching Him. Sin had fixed a great gulf between the Holy God and sinful man; no man was able to span that chasm. Jesus Christ is the bridge between us and God. Jacob in his dream saw the ladder which was not only in his father's tent, but also with the exile from his father's home in the lonely desert. That ladder reached to heaven (Gen. 28 : 12). Need we wonder that he called the name of that place Bethel, the house of God? Jesus Christ is the ladder between God and us. That ladder is not too short, nothing need be added to it. It reaches Father's heart in heaven. "There is one God, and *one mediator between God and men*, the man Christ Jesus" (1 Tim. 2 : 5). The curtains of goats' hair.

Divine Forgiveness, the curtains of goats' hair also speak to us. The goat which the Lord had destined to be the scapegoat was brought to the altar. The high priest laid both his hands upon its head, all the sins of his people which had been atoned by the blood. We can imagine the solemn hush as the people listened to this awful recital. A man is waiting to lead it into the desert. The crowd gives way to him; it opens its rows and gives him a broad passage. Their hearts beat more freely. That goat will never come back. *All the sins* of God's children are cast into the depths of the sea (Mic .7: 19). The sea will give up the dead which are in it, but never the sins of God's children covered by the blood of the lamb. "Thou hast in love to my soul delivered it from the pit of corruption: for thou hast cast all my sins behind thy back" (Isa. 38: 17). God always goes forward in His course; He never goes back.

We do not wonder now that the curtain had an extra length and that the sixth curtain in the forefront of the tabernacle had *to be doubled.* Everyone could see that Israel had received from the Lord's hand double for all her sins, if she would only accept it. If in the East, a reckoning was paid, it was folded double and a nail fastened through it as a sign that it had been paid. Curtains of goats' hair, you bring us good news. You speak to us of our heavenly Father. "As far as the east is from the west, so far hath he removed our transgressions from us" (Ps. 103: 12). "Comfort ye, comfort ye my people, saith your God. Speak ye comfortably to Jerusalem, and cry unto her, that her warfare is accomplished, that her *iniquity is pardoned*; for she hath received of the Lord's hand *double for all her sins*" (Isa. 40: 1, 2).

Scapegoat, as we follow thee in our thoughts in the desert, we shall never forget that *Christ was made sin* for us. As the high priest transferred the transgressions of the people to thy head and thou didst become so identified with them that thou didst become unclean, and the man who led thee away in the desert had to be cleansed; so our sins met in Christ. He took them upon Himself; He stood before God as though in some mysterious way they had become His own, and God who justifieth, who *declares* us *just*, the ungodly (Rom. 4: 5), has accepted us in His beloved Son. Our God will *abundantly pardon* (Isa. 55: 7).

But God is not only merciful and of great goodness, but He is also just. He loves the sinner, but cannot leave sin unpunished. In olden times a king had published a severe edict against adultery. Anyone found guilty should have both his eyes stuck out. The first culprit was his own son. What will the old king do? If he were to spare his own son, the feeling of justice amongst his people would have been wounded for many ages. The father was the judge, but the judge was the father. "However it may hurt me," he said, "I dare not act against the law of the kingdom. The punishment is the loss of both eyes. Stick out one of my eyes and one of my son's." The father was just, but he was also merciful. Our Saviour has done far more. He did not say, "I will bear half the punishment, and the sinner the other half." No, He took the whole burden of our sins upon Himself. Curtains of goats' hair, you speak to us of the love, the everlasting love, of our heavenly Father and of the substitutionary suffering of our Redeemer.

"God was in Christ, reconciling the world unto himself, not imputing their trespasses unto them; and hath committed unto us the word of reconciliation. Now then we are ambassadors for Christ, as though *God* did beseech you by us: we pray you in Christ's stead, be ye reconciled to God" (2 Cor. 5: 19, 20).

16

THE TABERNACLE OF FINE TWINED LINEN

1. Thou shalt make the tabernacle with ten curtains of fine twined linen, and blue, and purple, and scarlet: with cherubims of cunning work shalt thou make them.—EXODUS 26: 1

I HAD been spending some happy days in the home of a dear child of God. She had belonged to society and had been active in social work. Since she had found Christ her life had been completely changed. She had found other friends and other aims. Her daughter, a charming girl of eighteen, had not yet given her heart to the Saviour. This was hard for both. In life's most important questions they did not understand each other. I had asked her to go with me for a walk. We chatted together for some time. I asked her if she would not like to be a Christian. She gave me a straightforward answer: "I should like to be like Mother, for she is certainly happy, but you see I am still so young and when I become religious I have to give up so many things!"

I could not blame the child; she saw only the badgers' skin covering; she had never seen the beautiful coloured curtains. They can only be seen from the inside. Of course, I told her, it was not a question at all of giving up pleasant things, but of receiving. What a joy it was to me after a few months to receive a letter from her saying that Christ had found her and was her best friend, and that now she was the happiest girl in the world.

There are a great many people like my young friend. They only see the black roof of badgers' skins and believe that Christ's followers are all sad people. Why, Christianity was ushered into the world with a song and ends with the marriage of the Lamb. "Behold, I bring you tidings of great joy, which shall be to all people." I have had a long life and met a great many people on my travels. Many have opened their hearts to me. I may tell you, real Christians are the most joyful people I have met; they have a joy unspeakable, full of glory, a joy that is not depending on the state of the exchange or the weather, neither on good health, but finds its source in the Lord Jesus and He is the same yesterday, today and forever.

There are Christians, too, that have never advanced beyond the altar of burnt-offering and an occasional visit to the laver. They have taken from Christ forgiveness of their sins, but they have never fully yielded their lives to Christ. They have not gone on to know the Lord. They remained in the court and have never seen the beautiful curtains. The more we get to know the Lord, the more we shall grow in our inner life. "Grow in grace and in the knowledge of the Lord Jesus Christ" (2 Pet. 3: 18). Many Christians remain babies all their lives. When we do not go forward, we go back. Many Christians do not grow because they know the Lord so little.

What a wonderful sight for the priest who entered the sanctuary! Outside, the dark blue badgers' skins; inside, the golden walls, the ceiling of white twined linen woven with blue, purple and scarlet, figures of cherubim interwoven by skilful weavers, shining and reflecting in the light of the seven-armed candlestick; and this all is only a reflection of the beauty and majesty of our Saviour. Do we wonder that David says: "Thou art fairer than the children of men: grace is poured into thy lips: therefore God hath blessed thee forever" (Ps. 45: 2).

The ceiling as well as the vail and the gate to the court were made of the same material, the warp being of the very finest pure white yarn and the weft dyed blue, purple and scarlet. Wise women were the spinners (Exod. 35: 25), and wise men the weavers (Exod. 38: 8). The skins and curtains as a whole are called the tabernacle in Hebrew, the dwelling-place; the coverings of rams' skins dyed red and the badgers' skins were called the tent; but when regarded separately, the ceiling with the coloured curtains interwoven with cherubim was specially named the Tabernacle.

In studying the explanation of the interior of the tabernacle as the Holy Spirit gives us in Hebrews 10, we see that the inner vail of the tabernacle separating the Holy of holies from the sanctuary is a type of our Saviour as He lived in this world, the incarnate Son of God (Heb. 10: 20). That vail was rent in twain when our Lord gave up the ghost. No human hand could have done this for it was rent in twain from the top to the bottom (Matt. 27: 51). *Christ has rent the vail.* He has opened the way into the Holiest. We need not wait till we depart to be where Christ is; we may have that life in heaven even when we are still pilgrims on earth. Heaven is where God is, and God is omnipresent. God is where His children are. Father Laurard had this practice of the presence of God. He believed God was with him when he was washing dishes as well as when he was tending the sick. Oh, the blessedness of such a life in the holiest! May the Holy Spirit make it the habit of our soul to live in God's presence. Let us have boldness to go through the rent vail. I cannot but think it was Father that caused the vail to be rent. He longs for His children. He wants them always to abide with Him.

We have been standing looking at the vail as the light of the candlestick was shining upon it: Christ living, suffering and dying for us. Now let us lift up our eyes and look at the ceiling of white linen resplendent in its colours of blue, purple and scarlet. We see in it a type of the *risen Christ ascended* into heaven, the *glorified Christ* sitting on the right hand of the Father. When we read Exodus 26: 1, 31 carefully and compare them we notice that in the ceiling the order is fine linen, blue, purple and scarlet; in the gate of the court and the inner vail: blue, purple, scarlet, and fine linen last. The Holy Spirit has been pleased, in describing the ceiling, to draw our attention first to the white twined linen: the sinlessness, the spotlessness and holiness of Him that sat on the right hand of God in glory. When we enter the court, the Holy Spirit in teaching us to know Christ directs faith to look at the blue colour first. "And without controversy great is the mystery of godliness: God was *manifest* in the flesh." He came from heaven, He lived heaven on earth, and He went up to heaven. This is what the heavenly blue on the ceiling teaches. There is more. "He was justified in the Spirit, seen of angels, preached unto the Gentiles, believed on in the world, received up into glory" (I Tim. 3: 16). Surely great is the mystery of godliness. He is received into glory. The risen Christ, sitting at the right hand of the Father, is the same Saviour who lived, suffered, and died on earth. "Jesus Christ the same yesterday, and today and forever" (Heb. 13: 8). It is the same Jesus who died on the cross, who rose the third day, and whom the disciples saw going up into heaven. He still wears the scars on hands and feet.

In meditating on the different coverings: the badgers' skins, the rams' skins dyed red, the goats' skins, we have seen what Christ has done for us, how He has suffered for us, and how through Him we have remission of sins and all benefits of His passion.

On the ceiling we see first the white linen, the Son of God, the Lamb of God without spot. Our faith learns to look away from the gifts to the Giver. Although it is now many years ago, I still remember how my heart was once thrilled with joy. I often had to speak at conferences in different parts of Europe, and I always tried to bring some small present to the children on coming back. If I came back late at night, they were sure to get up early to welcome me and my suitcase. I never liked to come empty-handed. But then, somehow, a painful thought came into my heart. I felt there was a danger of the boys looking for the present rather than for me. I told them the next time I had to leave them that this time I should not bring them anything. I was away for a fortnight and longed to be home, and I felt sorry that I had told the children that this time I should not bring back anything. When I got near to home, I wondered whether the children would be waiting for me. I had nothing for them. I nearly felt tempted to go back to town and buy something for them. The nearer to home, the heavier my heart. Would they be glad that Father is back even when he has nothing to give them? I was wrong. They ran to meet me, and when I told them I had nothing for them this time, my little laddie jumped in my arms and said, "Dad, I love you all the same even when you do not bring us anything." How my heart rejoiced. The many-coloured ceiling teaches us that Christ is worth while to be loved by us apart from what He gives us. He is the altogether lovely one. A. B. Simpson experienced this when he wrote:

> Once it was the blessing,
>   Now it is the Lord.
> Once it was the feeling,
>   Now it is the Word.
> Once His gifts I wanted,
>   Now Himself alone.
> Once it was power I yearned for,
>   Now the Mighty One.

The four different colours show us four glorious traits in our Lord.

The *white linen* speaks of the stainless purity of our mediator. Saint Peter, who lived three years in close association with the Master, testified: "He did no sin, neither was guile found in his mouth." And he was willing for his beloved Master not only to suffer hardship, but to be crucified.

The *blue* is the colour of heaven. "No man hath ascended up to heaven, but he that came down from heaven, even the Son of man which is in heaven" (John 3: 13). Have you ever noticed in reading the Gospels how often Christ's thoughts dwelt in His Father's home and with His Father? Blue reminds us also of His heavenly character. His meet was to do the will of His Father and to seek His glory.

Purple is the colour for *His royal character.* He is the King's Son, before Him all kings shall fall down; all nations shall serve Him. He shall have dominion also from sea to sea, and from the river unto the ends of the earth (Ps. 72). In the annunciation the angel said to the virgin: "He shall be great, and shall be called the Son of the Highest: and the Lord God *shall give unto him the throne of his father David*: and he shall reign over the house of Jacob forever; and of his kingdom there shall be no end" (Luke 1: 32, 33). Has not the word of the angel been fulfilled? "He shall save his people from their sins." Dare we doubt that these latter promises shall also have their literal fulfilment? The purple shall be on His shoulder. And the beautiful hymn, shall it not soon find its fulfilment?

> Jesus Christ shall reign victorious,
> All the earth shall own His sway.

Scarlet reminds us of our Lord's passion. In some passages the Hebrew word for scarlet is translated by "worm." "I am a worm, and no man; a reproach of men, and despised of the people" (Ps. 22: 6). To understand the meaning of the word "scarlet" read Psalm 22 on your knees, and let the Holy Spirit speak to you through it. It is the most graphic description of the crucifixion: the bones out of joint, the intense suffering, the action on the heart (verse 14); the extreme thirst (verse 15); the hands and feet pierced; the parting of the garments. And all this for you and for me. The desolate cry in the verse, "My God, my God, why hast thou forsaken me?"; the exultant, "He hath done this," the Hebrew equivalent for the words, "It is finished." At the close, during those hours of agony and anguish, the meditation of our dying Saviour finished the ceremonial law, the vail rent in twain finished the fulfilment of prophecy; He finished the work which was given Him to do. He finished the work of atonement. As the Substitute and sin-bearer, the second Adam, sins of the race met on Him, but when He died, He put them away by the sacrifice of Himself. The scapegoat bore them into the land of forgetfulness from which they can never be recovered. The demand of divine justice was satisfied. Mercy and truth had met. Righteousness and peace embraced. And the cry of a finished redemption shall be finally crowned by a cry of complete restitution. "*It is done*" (Rev. 21 : 6).

In the four Gospels, which also give us four different aspects of our Lord, we find again these four colours: white linen, blue, scarlet and purple. *Saint Matthew* shows us the *purple,* the promised Messiah, the Son of David, the King of the Jews, the fulfilment of prophecy. Saint Mark shows us the *scarlet,* the Servant of Jehovah who went about doing good, who had come not to be ministered unto but to minister and give His life a ransom for many.

Saint Luke shows us the *white twined* linen, the perfect Son of man, belonging to the whole human race, who had come to seek and find that which was lost. *Saint John* on eagle's wings lifts our soul on high and shows us the *heavenly blue,* the Son of God. He wanted to show us not chiefly what our Lord had done, but what He was in Himself. He gives us a deep insight into the inner life of our Lord. In the heavenly blue he shows us how the Word was *made flesh* and *dwelt* among us "and we beheld His glory (the glory as of the only begotten of the Father), *full of grace* and *truth*" (John 1: 14).

White, blue, purple and scarlet, but all four blended together. There was a balance, a consistency in our Lord's character which made Him unique.

Some time ago a sentence struck me in a book I was reading: *"Our Lord was musical."* Surely the gracious words which fell from His lips had a sweetness of tone all of its own, and when the disciples sang the "Hallelujah" at the close of the Passover to the honour of God the Father, I am sure He did not keep silent, but joined them in the hymn of praise. Singing, He went to Gethsemane. In another aspect we might say our Lord was musical. In Him all was harmony. His whole life was harmony, a symphony to the glory of His Father. When we study our Lord's life, no trait of character pushed the others in the background. When I study Peter's character there are traits in it I like; he was so human. If I study Saint John's character there is much that attracts me. In our Lord all was consistent, all attractive, all lovely, all harmony.

Figures of cherubim were interwoven by skilful workmen, it may be by Bezaleel and Aholiab, who had been filled with the Spirit of God in all manner of workmanship. They are God's ministering servants, sent out to do His pleasure. Cherubim, no longer with a flaming sword as at the gates of Eden, but with outspread wings, greeted the worshipper as he entered the holy place. They speak to us of the mighty power of Him who has said: "All power is given unto me in heaven and in earth" (Matt. 28: 18).

In whatever direction the priest looked, everywhere he saw the wings of the cherubim. Under the shadow of those wings he felt perfectly safe. I too, as a member of His body, king and priest, may make my refuge *in the shadow of God's wings* until these calamities be overpast (Ps. 57: 1), and praise Him: "Because thou hast been my help, therefore in the *shadow of thy wings* will *I rejoice*" (Ps. 63: 7). "He that dwelleth in the secret place of the most High, shall abide under the shadow of El-shaddai, the all-sufficient one." The terror by night, the pestilence that walketh in darkness will have no terror for you. Reader, do you abide in the secret place of the most High? We are living in ominous times. Many hearts tremble with fear, but your heart is fixed. You know that adversities are the shadows of the wings of the all-sufficient One. He is never nearer to His children than when they need Him most.

A little boy with large, dark eyes, a pallid face, was lying on the operating table. The old doctor put his hand on the heart as the nurse was administering the chloroform. He was pausing a moment; his eyes lifted upwards before he took the knife. How he longed with God's help to save the little life. "Is he under the chloroform?" As he took the knife, the boy was singing softly:

> Safe in the arms of Jesus,
>   Safe on His gentle breast,
> There by His love o'ershadowed,
>   Sweetly my soul shall rest.

That little laddie was in the sanctuary under the protection of the wings of the Almighty.

White twined linen curtain! you speak to me of Him whose name is the Lord, our Righteousness (Jer. 23: 6). Do you know, reader, that the name of your King will be yours also? "They shall call them, The holy people, The redeemed of the Lord" (Isa. 62: 12). "He hath clothed me with the garments of salvation; he hath covered me with the robe of righteousness." This is our present privilege. Here on earth already we are accepted in the Beloved, having on the breastplate of righteousness (Eph. 6: 14), and when you love His appearing, the Lord will give you a crown of righteousness (2 Tim. 4: 8). Then no spot will be found any more on your garment. Your garments will always be white, and your head will not lack in oil" (Eccles. 9: 8).

"Now we see through a glass, darkly; but then face to face: now I know in part; but then shall I know even as also I am known" (1 Cor. 13: 12).

17

THE LAMB IS ITS LIGHT

And the city had no need of the sun, neither of the
moon, to shine in it: for the *glory* of God did lighten
it, and the *Lamb is the light thereof.*
— REVELATION 21 : 23

AN old sea captain told at a convention in Holland
that he had lately found the Saviour on his journey
out to the Indies. So great was his joy that he wished
all his friends to share it. But how to set about doing
this seemed rather difficult to him. At last he had a
brainy idea. When he arrived in Batavia he bought a
parrot and on the journey home he spent a good deal of
his time in his cabin with his parrot. It did not seem
quite clear to me at the time what the parrot had to
do with his conversion. It soon became clear, however.
When any of the captain's old friends knocked at his
door, the parrot answered, "Come in!" When once they
were well inside, he greeted them with the question,
"Are you converted? Then it is all right."

The old captain's heart was better than his theology
and his method of soul-winning. It is not all right with
us when we are converted. Conversion is not the end,
but the beginning of your Christian life. God wants to
train you and make something out of you to the praise
of His glory. You were predestinated for this (Eph. 1:
5, 6). When the king adopts a little child from the

155

slums, he first takes away its filthy rags and clothes it with the garment of salvation. But surely this is not all. The child has to become fit for the royal palace. It has so much to learn and so much to unlearn. He sends it to school. With infinite patience Father Himself trains you. For this is your story—Conversion not the end, but the beginning of your Christian life.

We have gone together through the court of the tabernacle. A long time we stopped at the brazen altar of burnt-offering. As we watched the lamb that was slain, we saw how at infinite cost Christ on the rugged cross bore our sins, and as His eyes looked with compassionate love down upon us, He asked us: "So much I did for thee, what doest thou for me?" And this question called forth a response in our grateful hearts. A friend wrote a most helpful booklet for young Christians. Its title may not be the best English, but it certainly was sound theology. Its title was: "Christ for Me—Me for Christ!"

As we continued our way, we stopped at the brazen laver made out of the Egyptian mirrors the women gladly gave. We learned the necessity of daily cleansing. Father made gracious provision for the cleansing of His children's feet when covered with the dust of the earth, or hands stained in working.

But, dear friends, shall we stay in the court? Amaziah, the king of Judah, had hired a hundred thousand valiant men of Israel to help him in his war with Edom. This cost him a hundred talents. A prophet warned him against this unholy alliance and urged him to send the men back to Israel. The king ruefully was thinking about his hundred talents. The prophet's answer was that we never are losers if we give up something for the Lord.

"The Lord is able to give thee much more than this" (2 Chron. 25: 9). "The path of the just is as the shining light *that shineth more and more* unto the perfect day." Father calls His children to a life of fellowship with Him in the sanctuary. He has made us kings and priests. Every child of God is called to service as a priest, and as a priest he has like Elijah to stand before God, to cultivate the consciousness of God's presence.

No sunbeam could penetrate into the sanctuary. The covers of badgers' skins, rams' skins, goats' skins which, with the white twined linen, formed the roof of the tabernacle did not let a single ray of sunshine through. The light of nature cannot light up the tabernacle. Just as impossible as it is for a blind man to admire the variegated colours of the autumn landscape, just as impossible it is for the natural man to comprehend the divine: *"The natural man* receiveth not the things of the Spirit of God: for they are foolishness unto him: *neither can he know them,* because they are spiritually discerned" (1 Cor. 2: 14).

It would be a great mistake, however, to think that the tabernacle was developed in gloom and darkness. The priest had no need to tap about in darkness. The seven-armed candlestick sheds its light in every direction and was reflected on the golden walls of the sanctuary. The wonderful brilliance of colour, blue, red, and scarlet on a background of gold, must have offered a wonderful spectacle to the priest looking on of which outsiders could have no conception.

"The Lord shall be unto thee an everlasting light,

and thy God thy glory" (Isa. 60: 19). Our Lord Jesus Christ is the golden candlestick. He is the glory of God, the brightness of His glory, and the express image of His person (Heb. 1: 3). Even when He came in humiliation, He could say, "I am the light of the world" (John 8: 12), and now as the glorified head of His body, the church, He is at the right hand of the Father, and heaven and earth are full of His glory. "The city had no need of the sun, neither of the moon, to shine in it: for the *glory of God* did lighten it, and the *Lamb is the light thereof*" (Rev. 21: 23).

The golden candlestick was the only light in the sanctuary; no other light was allowed. Where our Lord is the light, all other lights empale. Even heaven itself would be a dark place if our Lord were not there.

Moody tells the story of a little child who was brought to stay with an aunt when the mother was dying. The child wanted Mother and begged to be taken home. But Mother had gone to Father's home with the many rooms. The child wandered from room to room, crying for Mother. No answer came. She went back to the door. They asked the little one where she wanted to go. The answer was right, "Home to Mother, where Mother lives." Where there is no mother, there is no home, and where our Lord is not there is no heaven. God's children have heaven on earth; they may sit here already with Christ in heavenly places.

As a little boy, I tried to see if I could reach the horizon. The further I went, the further went the horizon. I thought then that heaven and God must be far away. Heaven is not so far away as most people think. It all depends on how near our heart is to God. Jacob could rest on a stone in the desert, Daniel in the lion's den, Peter in prison, John in the isle called Patmos. They could not change their circumstances, but they could determine their atmosphere. Around John there was a large circle called Patmos, but there was an inner circle around him. He was in the Spirit, in Patmos. All four had a bit of heaven around them and each child of God should have the same. Each house in which a child of God lives might be a Bethany. Our Lord said: "If a man love me, he will keep my words: and my Father will love him, and we will come unto him, and make our abode with him" (John 14: 23).

The Golden Candlestick

18

THE GOLDEN CANDLESTICK

31. And thou shalt make a candlestick of *pure* gold: of *beaten* work shall the candlestick be made: his *shaft,* and his *branches,* his *bowls,* his knops, and his flowers, shall be of the same.

32. And six branches shall come out of the sides of it; *three* branches of the candlestick out of the one side, and three branches of the candlestick out of the other side:

33. *Three* bowls made like unto almonds, with a knop and a flower in one branch; the *three* bowls made like almonds in the other branch, with a *knop* and a *flower*: so in the six branches that come out of the candlestick.

34. And in the candlestick shall be *four* bowls made like unto almonds, with their knops and their flowers.

35. And there shall be a knop under two branches of the same.

37. And thou shalt make the *seven lamps* thereof: and they shall *light* the lamps thereof, that they may give light *over against it.*—EXODUS 25: 31-35, 37

As we enter the sanctuary, it is but natural that our eyes are first directed towards the golden candlestick. Without its burning light the sanctuary would have been full of darkness and gloom. It was of *pure* gold; all the other furniture of the tabernacle, the table of shewbread, the altar of incense, the ark, were made of acacia wood overlaid with gold. The mercy seat and the golden candlestick were of pure gold. Its value must have been at least thirty thousand dollars. We notice that the centre shaft rises above the branches. It had four bowls in the shape of almonds with their knops and their flowers, whereas the branches have only *three* bowls with a knop and a flower in one branch.

The *golden candlestick* is a *wonderful symbol* of the *union between Christ and His disciples.* Our Lord is centre shaft. We are His branches. More even than this, our Lord is not only the shaft, but He is *the candlestick* itself. (Exod. 25: 34). "And in the candlestick were four bowls made like almonds, his knops, and his flowers" (Exod. 37: 20). As the branches are part of the tree, so are we joined to our Lord. The candlestick had flowers and knops. Our Lord used a similar type: when on His way to Gethsemane, pointing to a vine, He drew their attention to the close union between them. "I am the vine, ye are the branches" (John 15: 5). "For as the body is one, and hath many members, and *all* the members of that *one body, being many,* are *one* body: *so also is Christ*" (1 Cor. 12: 12).

Branches and candlestick are one. Our Lord does not say: "I am the stem of the vine, ye are the branches." He says: "I am the vine itself. Separated from the vine, the branch is valueless. The joiner has no use for it. It is no use even as a nail to hang something on. It is only good for firewood and little good for that (Ezekiel 15: 3–4).

Six branches shall come out of the sides of it (Exod. 37: 21). Is six a perfect number? No, it denotes incompleteness. It is only when the branches are joined to the shaft that we get the perfect number seven. Separated, *apart* from the shaft, they would not even be able to stand upright, in fact they would have no standing, no right to be in the sanctuary at all.

Am I sorry because I am entirely depending on my Saviour? On the contrary, there is no happier life than the branch-life. I need not try to find nourishment for myself; the vine is responsible for it. I need not even try to hold myself. The vine carries the branch. May I come to you, Master, not only for guidance in important decisions in my life and work; may I also come to you with the little troubles of my daily life? You say that everything which interests me, also is of the greatest interest to you? That you like me to come and talk over with you all that has happened to me through the day, just as the disciples did when they came back from their mission? (Mark 6: 30). May I tell you everything? How can I ever thank you enough that you are prepared to play such an important part in my life? "Child, I am not only part of your life, *I am your life*. I am not the stem, I am the vine."

Is it not right that the shaft should rise above the branches and have four bowls instead of three? "God hath put all things under his feet and gave him to be the head over all things to the church, which is his body" (Eph. 1: 22, 23). Yes, shaft and candlestick are one and each of its rays tells us: "Apart from me ye can do nothing."

Each branch is not only joined to the shaft but also to the branch on the other side. The same gold that joined the branch on the left side of the shaft also unites the branch on the right side of it. God's children are all members of Christ, but also joint-members of each other—many members, one body. "The eye cannot say unto the hand, I have no need of thee" (1 Cor. 12: 21). My brother may have different opinions from mine on some points but I dare not forget that we are *"all one in Christ Jesus"* (Gal. 3: 28). We agree on far more points than we differ. Let our conversation be on what unites us, not what separates us. Let Christ be the subject of our conversation. We shall then receive a burning heart, burning in love to Christ and to my brother. When we stand in a circle and Christ is in His right place in the centre, the nearer each of us gets to Christ, the nearer we get to each other. The candlestick was of pure gold. We have noticed that the metal chiefly used in the court was copper; in the sanctuary, gold. Gold speaks of glory. Christ was pure gold. Dean Law said, "I rejoice in my all-gold Saviour."

Make the candlestick of pure gold of *beaten work*. The gold had to be on the anvil; it had to be hammered. "Ought not Christ to have suffered these things, and to enter into his glory?" (Luke 24: 26). Bethlehem cannot take the place of Golgotha. It is not through the incarnation that we become members of His body, but by His death and resurrection. "He was wounded for our transgressions. The Lord hath laid on him the iniquity of us all" (Isa. 53: 5, 6). The captain of our salvation was made perfect *through sufferings* (Heb. 2: 10). "Though he were a Son, yet learned he obedience by the things *which he suffered*" (Heb. 5: 8).

If we are to become Christ-like, we must go the same way the Saviour has gone. Paul counted no price too dear that he might know Christ and the power of His resurrection and the *fellowship of His sufferings*, and to be made conformable to His death (Phil. 3: 10). The shaft was of *beaten* gold; the branches too have to be of beaten gold. I heard a brother once give this testimony: "Christ bore His cross; I bear mine. We two belong together."

You have to be on the anvil. It is the only way to become beaten gold. When Moses was forty years old, he thought he could deliver his people. God could not use him then. He sent the man who was brought up in the king's palace, schooled in the wisdom of the Egyptians, into the lonely desert. There he was in God's school, forty years on the anvil.

God sent Samuel to anoint David king. He slew Goliath; he became the favourite of the people. Then God sent him into the cave of Adullam to be hammered on the anvil: Shadrach, Meshach and Abednego refused to bow down to the image of King Nebuchadnezzar. Daniel would worship only God. As a reward for their faithfulness they were put on the anvil, into the fiery furnace and the den of lions, but how they shone afterwards as branches of the candlestick. Father takes His children in His own training school. He does this often through our surroundings. When the Lord took Jacob in His training school He sent him to his Uncle Laban. He was a hard master. Those years with Laban were hard years. When Jacob had learned his lesson, God sent him back home.

It may be one of my readers has a Laban whom he finds trying. Even when you work in fellowship with other Christians for the Lord, whether at home or abroad, you may find one rather trying. Do not forget then that you are on the anvil. You are in God's school. He is going to make something out of you. Jacob would never have become Israel without a Laban. Have you ever thanked God for your Laban? This would be according to Scripture: *"Giving thanks always for all things* unto God and the Father in the name of our Lord Jesus Christ"* (Eph. 5: 20).

I know the heavy blows with the hammer are not always the most difficult to bear. For one thing, they are not of frequent occurrence and God gives special grace. The little, daily blows, the daily pin-pricks, may hurt even more.

I want to say two things for your comfort. I have been on the anvil myself. The hammer is all the time in Father's hands. He is the refiner who sits to test the silver, till it shows the silver look, till it reflects the Master's face.

Some of you may go through hard times just now. Blow after blow comes. Listen, every blow that falls on the branch also falls on the shaft. "We have *not an high priest which cannot be touched with the feeling* of our infirmities; but was in all points tempted as we are, yet without sin" (Heb. 4: 15).

19

SHINING FOR JESUS

2. Behold a *candlestick all of gold*, with a bowl upon the top of it, and his seven lamps thereon, and *seven pipes* to the seven lamps, which are upon the top thereof:

3. And *two olive trees* by it, one upon the right side of the bowl, and the other upon the left side thereof.

4. So I answered and spake to the angel that talked with me, saying, What are these, my Lord?

6. Then he answered and spake unto me, saying, This is the word of the Lord unto Zerubbabel, saying, *Not by might, nor by power, but by my spirit*, saith the Lord of hosts.—ZECHARIAH 4: 2-4, 6

THERE was no natural light in the tabernacle. In the sanctuary was the golden candlestick shedding its light upon the table of shewbread, the altar of incense, the vail, and throwing it upwards to the many-coloured ceiling. The Holy of holies was lit up by the shekinah, the manifested glory of God. "I am the light of the world: he that followeth me shall not walk in darkness, but shall have *the light of life*" (John 8: 12). The light of man, Christ, is the golden candlestick and sheds His light upon each member of His body. No child of God need grope in the dark. We are all the children of light (1 Thess. 5: 5). The pure olive oil beaten for the light, causes the *lamp to burn always* (Exod 27: 20). That light never goes out and hence "the path of the just is as the shining light, that *shineth* more and more unto the perfect day" (Prov. 4: 18). We are marching on to Zion, to the city of lights, where there is no need of sun or moon, because the Lamb is the light thereof.

We find the golden candlestick mentioned in the Bible when the tabernacle was built (Exod. 25: 31–40), in Revelation 1: 12, 20, and in Zechariah 4.

In our study of the tabernacle we have noticed that every type of Christ, the head of the body, must needs also to some extent be a type of the members of His body. So it is with the golden candlestick. Christ said not only, "I am the light of the world," but also, "Ye are the light of the world" (Matt. 5: 14).

When we meditate on the prophet's vision as a type of Christ and His church, we notice the large bowl upon the top containing the oil which was constantly supplied by the two olive trees on either side of the candlestick, and the seven pipes by which the oil reached the seven lamps.

I still remember the time when we had neither gas nor electricity in our home, but were depending on oil-lamps. They shed a comfortable homely light on the family gathered around the table. Most of my readers know little about lamps. I know something about them. For a burning lamp you need two things: first of all oil, and then a wick that is dipped into the oil.

Oil in Scripture, I hardly need remind my readers, is an emblem of the Holy Ghost. Priests, prophets and kings were anointed in the Old Testament dispensation and the anointing of our king is one of the most touching features in the coronation. Our Lord in His sermon at Nazareth quoted: "The *Spirit of the Lord* God is upon me; because the Lord hath *anointed* me to preach good tidings" (Isa. 61:1). To the mourners in Zion, the oil of joy is given for mourning (Isa. 61:3), and God anointed His Son with the *oil of gladness* (Heb. 1:9). The oil of the Holy Spirit. How we need the Holy Spirit for our life and ministry! Many years ago Dr. Andrew Murray wrote, "It is the will of God that *every* child of God should be filled with the Holy Spirit. Without the fullness of the Holy Spirit, no member of the body, no child of God can come up to Father's ideal for his life and his service. Every child of God has the Holy Spirit dwelling within him. It is, however, a different experience to be filled with the Holy Spirit." Surely this is the explanation for the rapid growth of the early church.

I am only a wick. How important it is to learn this lesson. With many of us it takes a long time before we have learned it. It is only when the wick is soaked with oil that it can burn. If it does not touch the oil, it produces soot and smoke. Sometimes the wick is screwed down too much. Many of God's children are satisfied to live on a low level. Sometimes the wick is too high and it emits nothing but soot. A room had to be redecorated; the wall-paper, the curtains were completely spoiled. If you wish for the fullness of the Holy Spirit in order that your church should be crowded and people flock to hear you, the Holy Spirit could not work through you. If people begin to talk about the wick, there is generally something wrong with the burning.

Now will you allow me to ask you a question, brother? Is your light burning brightly? "Lux lucet

ex tenebris" is the motto of the Waldensian Church.
Does your light shine in darkness? Your colleagues
in office and shop may not be Christians; they will
watch your life, your words, your actions. Are you
shining for Jesus?

> Keep me shining, Lord!
> Keep me shining, Lord!
> In all I say and do;
>> That the world may see
>> *Christ lives in me*
> And wants to love Him too.

You cannot accumulate the oil. We cannot live on
our past experiences, however precious they have been.
We need a fresh supply of oil each day. There is a
constant supply from the two olive trees. There is no
fear that the oil will be exhausted and the supply
may give out, however long you may burn. It is true
that "I can do all things through Christ that strengtheneth me" (Phil. 4: 13).

John the Baptist was a shining and burning light.
Shining is not the same as working. Living, being, is
more important than doing. The fullness of the Holy
Spirit is not only for service, for special occasions. In
one of our conventions a dear child of God was filled
with the Holy Spirit. She was asked some time afterwards if she had noticed any special results in her
work for the Lord. She paused before answering the
question and then said thoughtfully, "I cannot say that
I have; only I have won the heart of my children!"

The lamp must shine where the Master has put it.
Many a worker believes he would shine better if the
Lord would put him somewhere else. He feels a lack

of fellowship and doubts whether his people pray for him. I cannot tell, brother, if you would do better for the Lord elsewhere. I was reading again this morning Isaiah 53, the evangel in the Old Testament. It is said of the Lord: "For he shall grow up before him as a tender plant, and as a *root out of a dry ground.*" Our Lord could draw no nourishment from His surroundings. He lived in an atmosphere of doubt and misunderstanding. His own brothers did not believe in Him. He could not draw help from it, it was dry ground. Yet that tender plant grew. He drew His life from above, not from beneath. I have seen fir trees grow on rocks. Botany teaches there is an acid in the roots which penetrates the rock and makes room for the roots. They give before they take. Throughout our Lord's life He was always the giving one. When the Holy Spirit opens our eyes to the fact that we must give first, we cease to complain about our surroundings and it may be unconsciously we begin to shine and grow in dry ground.

Is your lamp burning brightly? It is very dark around us. No lamp can be spared. If your light is dim, you may cause someone to stumble. I had a fellow-student at college who was blind. When we dropped into his room after dinner, there were always two big candles burning. I asked him once if he did not consider this extravagance. He answered, "It is true I do not need them, but I do not want you fellows to stumble."

You may not be a big light, but God may use your little candle to lighten a big light. Did you ever notice that when John mentions Andrew, he always adds "the brother of Simon Peter." It seems to me always that John put this addition, thinking the reader may never have heard anything about Andrew, but everybody was sure to know Simon Peter. We know little of Andrew, only that he practised individual work. I can well imagine that when Andrew listened to that wonderful sermon at Pentecost, when three thousand were won for the Lord, he lifted up his heart in gratitude to the Lord that it was he who first found his brother Simon and led him to the Master. You may never be a Peter, but will you not be an Andrew?

You cannot accumulate oil; neither need you. There is a constant supply of oil dropping from the two olive trees into the bowl. There is no fear of the supply giving out. Christ is the accumulator. All we need, we have in him. "Apart from me, ye can do *nothing*" (John 15: 5). Keep on burning, the supply of oil will be commensurate to your burning. Shining and working are not the same. Being is more important than doing. The fullness of the Holy Spirit is not for special occasions only. We need to be constantly filled. You will not be when you seek your own honour. "Non nobis, non nobis"—All glory, laud, and honour to the Redeemer King. If our lamp burns, we owe it all to the shaft, and it will not burn any the brighter by putting other lamps into the shade.

What is the cause that many lamps do not burn brightly? Is our blessed Lord to blame? Is the Holy Spirit to blame? Is the supply of oil not sufficient? There may be *three causes* which keep the lamp from burning: (1) It may be that there is something wrong at the end of the wick; it does not reach into the oil;

(2) it is also possible that rust may have gathered at the top, or (3) that there is a knot somewhere in the wick which hinders the oil from rising to the top.

The wick no longer reaches into the oil. There is still some oil in the wick, but there is no fresh inflow. It may be the wick is not at once conscious of it; others may notice it first. Soon a disagreeable odour will draw people's attention to the wick. It always shows that there is something wrong when people talk about the wick. They never do when the lamp burns brightly. We are ambassadors for Christ. May Christ be glorified, not the ambassador. May we be effaced in our message. Does the wick no longer reach into the oil? Is there a lack of inflow? Dr. Chapman once told how he had a talk with Dr. F. B. Meyer at Northfield. He told him of the number of meetings at which he had spoken: how he was constantly giving out. I wonder if you have ever felt like that, brother? "Dr. Meyer laid his hand in a loving way on my shoulder and said to me," said Dr. Chapman, "'Brother, have you ever tried three times exhaling and once inhaling?'" Dr. Chapman said, "I felt a little annoyed. I fancied Dr. Meyer had misunderstood me altogether and was recommending me a new method of voice culture. However, to please the old man, I tried the experiment. I soon found out that it was impossible." You cannot exhale unless you have inhaled first. There must be inflow before there can be outflow. May I be allowed a question? What about your quiet time with the Master? What about your prayer life? Has the Lord been speaking to you this morning through His word? I do not mean in your family worship. I mean in the prayer closet. The Holy

Spirit was waiting to give you a private lesson this morning; why did you not come? You say you have studied your Bible this morning. You had to prepare a Bible-reading. Again I say, I did not mean that. The trouble with us preachers is that we read the Bible for others instead of for ourselves. Your Bible-reading will only be blessed when through the Word you are reading the Holy Spirit can speak personally to you. He will give you what you need for the day. The wick must touch the oil. You must be in touch with the Holy Spirit.

Rust may have collected at the top of the wick by the very burning. Is this possible? How often have I knelt down in my study after having preached or given a Bible-reading to ask the Lord to cover with His precious blood whatever was of self in the sermon I had just preached. Have you not felt the same? Our Father knows how weak the instruments are He is using, and in His mercy He provides snuffers and snuff-dishes and tongs of pure gold. So important the Lord considered that the lamps should burn brightly that He entrusted the golden snuffers only to the hands of the high priest. It is the husbandman Himself, our *heavenly Father*, who purgeth every branch that it may bear *more fruit* (John 15: 2).

There may be a knot somewhere in the wick. The oil cannot penetrate into the wick. This is a cause that so many prayers of God's children are not answered. There was a knot in Samson's wick. Delilah had entered into his life. Samson, the Nazarite, the man under a vow, gave his love and his heart to an unclean woman. She dragged him down and surrendered him to the

Philistines. Samson did not know that the Lord was departed from him (Judges 16: 20). "If I regard iniquity in my heart (if the motive of my prayer is not the Lord's glory but my own) the Lord will not hear me" (Ps. 66: 18). It may be that some one amongst my readers is conscious that there is not the power in his ministry there used to be. Be sure there is a knot somewhere in the wick and as long as the knot is there the oil cannot ascend. Our blessed Lord is a master in unravelling knots. Go straight to Him. He will understand all about it. He knows all about your knot; He was concerned about it. He can, however, do nothing for you until you come to Him and ask Him to untie your knot. He has such tender hands; He is so patient. I know it. There is restoring grace for you. "If *we confess* our sins, *he* is faithful and just to *forgive us* our sins and *to cleanse us* from *all* unrighteousness" (1 John 1: 9).

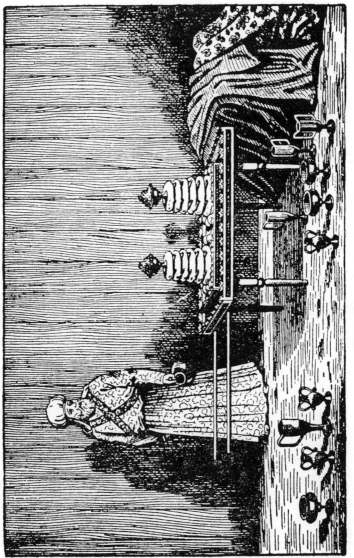

The Table of Shewbread

20

THE TABLE OF SHEWBREAD

23. Thou shalt also make a table of acacia wood: two cubits shall be the length thereof, and a cubit the breadth thereof, and a cubit and a half the height thereof.

26. And thou shalt make for it four rings of gold, and put the rings in the four corners that are on the four feet thereof.

27. Over against the border shall the rings be for places of the staves to bear the table.

30. And thou shalt set upon the table shewbread before me alway.—Exodus 25: 23, 26, 27, 30

In some of our watering-places, you will find on many houses a notice: "Rooms without board." As a rule the owners have large houses and are glad to let some of their rooms, but do not furnish meals to their guests. Our heavenly Father does not only provide for His children a dwelling-place; He wants to give His children a home and in a home a table is needed for the meals of the children.

In the sanctuary we have not only the golden candlestick but also the altar of incense and the table of shewbread. It is the royal table destined for the King. Joseph had three tables in his dining-hall: one for the Egyptians, one for his brethren, and one for himself (Gen. 43: 32). They served him by himself. Our King likes to see the happy faces of His children around

Him and bids them take a seat with Him at His table. "Behold, I stand at the door and knock: if any man hear my voice, and open the door, I will come in to him, and will *sup with him*, and *he with me*" (Rev. 3: 20).

The table was made of the acacia wood of the desert and overlaid with gold, and so points us to the twofold nature of our Saviour: His divine and His human nature. In Him, the Godhead and Manhood were joined together in one person, Christ. "As children partake of flesh and blood, he likewise took part of the same, that by death, he might destroy him who has the power of death, that is to say the devil" (Heb. 2: 14). Christ knew what it meant to be weary, to feel hungry and thirsty. It brings our Lord so near to us. He is able to feel with us. He had to take our human nature in order to expiate our sin by His death on the cross. He had to be divine to give that sacrifice its infinite value, a full-sufficient oblation and satisfaction for the sins of the whole world. "God was in Christ, reconciling the world to himself."

The dimensions of the table were small. It was three feet long, one and a half feet broad and three feet high. On it Aaron placed each Sabbath morning twelve cakes or loaves of equal size, in two rows, each representing one of the tribes. Those of the previous week had to be eaten by Aaron and his sons in the holy place.

Two names are given to these loaves. It was called *Bread of the Presence*; bread that could be placed before the King, royal bread. It was also called the *continual bread* (Num. 4: 7). The royal table is never empty. God calls His children to Him every moment. They need never be afraid to come to an empty table. Father calls the children: "Come, for all things are now ready" (Luke 14: 17).

The loaves were made from the finest flour. They are a type of Christ. Our Lord tells us so Himself. "I am *the bread of life*: he that cometh to me shall never hunger; and he that believeth on me shall never thirst" (John 6: 35). It is only as we are feeding on Him, we have life in us (John 6: 53).

The golden candlestick's light fell on the bread of the presence. The Father is well-pleased in His Son who gave His life a ransom for many, as typified by those two rows of cakes. Where Christ is, there are also His disciples; and so the Father is also pleased with His children, and even the weakest child is accepted in the beloved.

Every tribe had its loaf, not one failed. They were also of equal size. God looks at the branches of the church in a different way than we do. To us some of the loaves seem to be considerably larger than the others. We may even think that some of the tribes have no loaf at all on the table. God thinks differently. He looks at Christ and *in Him we are complete.*

Under the Old Testament dispensation only the priests were allowed to eat the bread. Under the new covenant all God's children belong to the royal priesthood and, therefore, every child has a right to a seat at the table, whether he belongs to the tribe of Judah or Benjamin, or any other tribe. It is not the table of Judah or Benjamin, but the King's table and He invites them all. It is very sad that the sacred legacy which Christ bequeathed to His Church as a continual memory of His sacrificial love, to give them food for their journey, should have become a cause of separation and division instead of witnessing to the world till Christ comes again of that sacred bond of love which unites His children not only to their Lord but also to each other.

"For we being many are one bread, and one body: for we are all partakers of that one bread" (1 Cor. 10: 17). When I look at the table of shewbread and see how close the loaves are one to another, I long for the time when Psalm 133: 1: "Behold, how good and how pleasant it is for brethren to *dwell together* in unity!" will be a reality.

You never need fear that the King will not be pleased to see you at His table. He sent a special invitation to you and a King's invitation is a command. Perhaps you may consider yourself unworthy of a place at the royal table. Mephibosheth was of royal descent. He lived in Lo-debar, the place where there was no bread. Besides, he was lame on both feet. David bade Mephibosheth to reside in his palace from love for his father, Jonathan. He did eat continually at the king's table for Jonathan's sake. It seems to me that our King has a special love for lame people. Jacob wrestled with the angel at Peniel. It was only after the angel had touched the hollow of his thigh that he had to give up his wrestling and could only cling to the angel. Then he received the blessing and a new name, and though halting upon his thigh, the sun rose upon the halting man. Lame people obtain the blessing by clinging, not by wrestling (Gen. 32: 31). Why did Mephibosheth have a seat at the royal table? It was not because of his own merit; it was for his father's sake, for Jonathan's sake. Read the touching story—2 Samuel 9: 13. Why are you, lame child of God, a welcome guest at the royal table? For Jesus' sake.

Of all the furniture of the tabernacle, the table of shewbread was the lowest. It was only about two feet high. You will hardly have such a low table in your house. There is no child so small that cannot sit at this table. The important thing is not to look at the table, but to take your seat. The King has made all preparations. It is for us to accept the invitation which He sent us: "Come for all things are now ready" (Luke 14: 17).

It is not enough to look at the table. The bread had to be eaten (Lev. 24: 9). How often Dr. Torrey at Montrose told us: "Meditate on the Word." The Bible tells us to meditate on the Word in the night-watches. I cannot commend too strongly to my readers to memorize passages of Scripture. Only a few days ago it was my privilege to visit a lady eighty-four years old who had been confined to her bed for several years. I was delighted to listen to her repeating one passage of Scripture after the other. A sleepless night will neither seem long nor wearisome to you if you meditate on the Word and have the Holy Spirit as your Teacher at your bedside.

Have you been to the Table today? Have you had your breakfast? As a rule, children, healthy children, do not forget mealtime. The dinner-bell is useful for the grown-ups, but the stomach is a good substitute for children. It is sad that in so many Christian families there is no family-altar any more, as there was in preceding generations. I once heard a startling statement at Massanetta Springs from Bishop Henderson in an address wherein he pleaded eloquently for regular family worship. He said that in a district-meeting of his church officials he asked how many of them came from homes in which there was family-worship. Ninety-five per cent held up their hands. He continued that when he went into the auditorium downstairs he repeated the same question to the young people; not five per cent held up their hands. The children of the church-workers in the church. I do not infer that the parents did not read their Bibles. I suppose they did, but not with their children. I have found the same sad state in many churches where I have ministered. I thank the Lord that a new start has been made by some excellent little publication with a short daily explanation of a Scripture-passage.

It is wonderful to go with your children to the table of shewbread, but you must not consider that this suffices. You must go alone as well. Father will want to speak to you in private. The Bible will be a blessing to you when it has a personal message for you for the day. Do not go away from your closet until you have received it. I am sure you will need it during the day.

It is a sad thing that theological students often occupy their time in reading books about the Bible rather than reading the Bible itself and consequently have an insufficient knowledge of the Bible. Better read the Bible than ten books about the Bible.

I repeat the same advice to every child of God. Devotional books and commentaries are a great help, but the best way to study the Bible is to let the Bible explain itself. Take time for your Bible. Study in the early morning if possible. Ask the Holy Spirit to teach you. Dig deep and God will give you the hidden treasures of darkness (Isa. 45: 3). Dig for yourself; your joy will be all the greater if you discover a special treasure which perhaps you never have seen before, although you might have many times passed over the same spot. Only babies require feeding with a spoon.

Healthy children, who live on the mountain-top in pure air and have plenty of exercise, are sure to have a good appetite. If we begin to find fault with our food, if we say with the children of Israel: "Wherefore have ye brought us up out of Egypt to die in the wilderness? for there is no bread, neither is there any water; and *our soul loatheth this light bread*" (Num. 21: 5), there is sure to be something wrong with our health. You better go to the good Physician and tell Him all about it. He will put you right.

You do not get filled by reading a cookery book. If you eat too many cookies, you lose your appetite. There is desire with many congregations for topical, social sermons, interesting sermons, but often there is little gospel in them. It is the old-fashioned gospel only which has the power of saving souls. Paul was not ashamed of it (Rom. 1: 16).

It is by the sincere milk of the Word that *people grow* (1 Pet. 2: 2). I belong to the plain people; give me plain food—that suits me best. "Tell me the story simply, as to a little child."

They shall eat it in the holy place (Lev. 24: 9). Every child of God should have a holy place where he can be alone with God. In our crowded cities that might appear to many a poor child of God an impossibility. Then follow Studdart Kennedy's advice he used to give his missions. He told his hearers to make a mental picture of their private prayer room. Well I remember the picture-room of the young daughter of a farmer. A little gable-room, looking out on the cornfields; the little table set ready for tea, a chair awaiting the Saviour. I am sure the Lord loved to enter that little room.

A young girl gave her heart to the Saviour. Her mother was afraid the girl would become religious and spoil her chance of a good marriage, and tried to stop her reading the Bible. The girl wanted food for her soul and asked the Lord to wake her every morning at six o'clock, and the Lord did. Half an hour in the morning spent with the Lord tunes your soul for the whole day. Moses' face shone when he had been alone with the Lord; so will yours.

The table of shewbread had four golden rings. It went through the desert, and even a wilderness is not a bad place for you when the Lord speaks comfortably to you (Hos. 2: 14). God can prepare a table before you in the presence of your enemies (Ps. 23: 5). He did it for David when he fled from Absalom. If you leave the holy place, take the holy table with you. If Martha had taken it with her into the kitchen she would not have grumbled at Mary. Take it not only into the kitchen, but take it with you into your office and shop. I thank the Lord for the Pocket-Testament League. It provides a wonderful method of winning souls for Christ. I have given away many New Testaments. I was on one of the liners and had preached on Sunday. Before we left the steamer a society girl came to me. She was the first at sports, the first at the dance. She thanked me for my sermon. I looked at her rather surprisedly. Tears were in her eyes as she answered my unspoken thought. "That life does not satisfy," she said. I asked her if I might give her something to remind her of our voyage and showed her one of those beautiful New Testaments. I told her, however, that I could only give it to her under two conditions. "Will you promise to read some portion of it every day?" She gladly promised. I smiled as I told her my second condition. "Could you promise to take this little book with you wherever you go?" She thought a moment. "It is an awkward book at times, it may begin to talk." She took it. "I can manage," she said. "Give *ye* them to *eat*" (Mark 6: 37). I have never seen that girl since. I hope I shall some day. "Cast thy bread upon the waters: for thou shalt find it after many days" (Eccles. 11: 1).

The Altar of Incense

21

THE ALTAR OF INCENSE

1. And thou shalt make an altar to burn incense upon: of *acacia wood* shalt thou make it.

2. A cubit shall be the length thereof, and a cubit the breadth thereof; foursquare shall it be: and two cubits shall be the height thereof: the horns thereof shall be of the same.

3. And thou shalt *overlay it with pure gold,* the top thereof, and the sides thereof round about, and the horns thereof; and thou shalt make unto it *a crown of Gold round about.*

4. And *two golden rings shalt thou make to it under* the crown of it, by the two corners thereof, upon the two sides of it shalt thou make it; and they shall be for *places for the staves to bear it* withal.

6. And thou shalt put it *before the vail* that is by the ark of the testimony.—Exodus 30: 1-4, 6

"WHAT wilt thou that I should do unto thee?" Twice the Lord addresses this question to different persons. In Mark 10: 51 it is a blind beggar who, outside the gates of Jericho, appeals to the Lord for help. "Son of David, have mercy on me." A noisy crowd surrounds the Lord. Yet the cry for mercy reaches the Lord's compassionate heart. It always does. He bids blind Bartimaeus come to Him. What do you wish me to do for you? The Lord likes us to be definite in our requests. Master, my request is large, very large. It needs a miracle. Give me back my sight! Straightway the Lord

grants the request. The miracle is performed. Bartimaeus receives his sight.

In Matthew 20: 21, it is a mother with her two sons
standing before the Lord. She is the wife and mother
of fishermen. Many a time they have resolutely braved
the storm. Now they are hesitating; it seems as if one
looks to the other to proffer request. The Lord feels
they have some wish in their hearts. He always feels it.
To encourage them He puts the same question to them:
"What would you have me to do?" It is the mother
who comes to the rescue. "Grant that my sons may sit,
the one on thy right hand and the other on thy left,
when thou comest into thy kingdom."

It was a mother, ambitious for her sons. Many mothers
are. You say it was a foolish request. You are right.
There is no room for self on the throne near Jesus. It
is only when self is on the cross that Jesus is on the
throne. The disciples thought so too. The Lord saw
different. He saw behind the foolish request the great
faith that could greet Him as the coming King. It is
ever so. The little girl is fond of flowers and fond of
father. She loves to gather flowers for father's writing-
desk; before they reach the father's table, the mother
takes out the weeds, adds some of her own flowers and
tastefully arranges them—the child's flowers arranged
by mother. That is exactly what our high priest does
with our prayers. Through the heart of Jesus leads the
way to Father's heart. In all our afflictions He is afflicted.
He feels with you. How often we come to Father with
a foolish request. What a comfort it is to know that
every sigh, every wish, every prayer has to pass through
the heart of our loving Saviour.

At the altar of incense the Lord meets each one of us each day with the question: "What would ye have me do?" He adds to it the promise: "Whatsoever ye shall ask the Father in my name, he will give it you" (John 16: 23).

The altar of incense was foursquare; eighteen inches was its length and breadth; its height was three feet. It was made of acacia wood and overlaid with pure gold, signifying the twofold nature of Christ. The acacia wood points to His humility, the pure gold to His divinity.

"The Word was made flesh" (John 1: 14). Seventy-seven times in the New Testament we find the Lord calling Himself the Son of man. While we love to meditate on our Lord as the only-begotten of the Father full of grace and truth, it brings Him close to us when we think of Him as the Son of man. When we come home weary of a day's work we know that our Saviour can feel with us. He was weary of the journey (John 4: 6), sought rest in sleep (Matt. 8: 24), knew what it meant to be hungry (Matt. 21: 18), and thirsty (John 19: 28). He suffered (Luke 22: 44), and died (1 Cor. 15). Of His own free-will He emptied Himself of His glory (Phil. 2: 6) and had, therefore, to increase in wisdom (Luke 2: 52).

Even now in glory, He is God-Man. He rose from the dead with a glorified body. Stephen saw the Son of man in glory standing at the right hand of the Father (Acts 7: 56). He will come again and we shall see the Son of man coming in the clouds of heaven (Matt. 26: 64).

The acacia wood is overlaid with pure gold. His

apostles called Him the holy child Jesus (Acts 3: 14; 4: 27). Even demons gave testimony to His glory (Mark 1: 24; Luke 4: 34). A French proverb says: "A king is not a king to his personal attendants." The disciples lived with the Lord three years under the most various circumstances. What do they say about their Master? Peter says: "Who did no sin, neither was guile found in his mouth" (1 Pet. 2: 22). John says: "In him is no sin" (1 John 3: 5), and both sealed their testimony by a martyr's death. The altar of incense was overlaid with fine gold.

In our blessed Lord the human and divine were inseparably blended. "In that day shall the branch of the Lord be beautiful and glorious." The word "Zemach" is used of the Messiah. A branch partakes of the nature of the tree. The branch of the Lord points to Christ's divine nature. "And the fruit of the earth shall be excelled and comely for them that are escaped of Israel" (Isa. 4: 2)—the fruit of the earth pointing to His humanity.

Both the altar of burnt-offering and the altar of incense point to Christ. The vessels in the court of the tabernacle point to what Christ has done for us on earth. Those in the holy place show us what Christ is now doing for His Church in heaven, where He is in glory sitting at the right hand of the Father. "Who *delivered* us from so great a death, and *doth deliver*: in whom we trust that he *will yet deliver us*" (2 Cor. 1: 10). *He hath delivered* points to His work on earth. It is finished, a full, complete sacrifice, oblation, and satisfaction for the sins of the whole world.

He *doth deliver.* This points to Christ's work for us as our high priest in the holy place, praying for us ever living to make intercession for us (Heb. 7: 25), delivering us from the habit and dominion of sin.

We trust He *will yet deliver* us, points to a glorious future when we shall have a redeemed body. Salvation is in three tenses. Salvation in the past from the guilt and penalty of sin; salvation in the present, being saved from the habit and dominion of sin; salvation in the future, the redemption of the body. "We know that when he shall appear we shall be *like him.*" In the court we look up to the crucified Saviour, the Lamb of God that beareth the sins of the world. In the holy place we meet the glorified Saviour, but He is the same Jesus yesterday, today and forever. Both altars had four horns to cling to. There is power, wonderful power, in the blood for forgiveness and cleansing. In the power of His risen life we find the power for a life of victory day by day. He is our life.

Both altars had rings, both were of acacia wood, those in the court overlaid with brass, those in the holy place covered with gold. Both altars had staves which were inserted in the rings. The tabernacle and its vessels accompanied Israel in their travellings in the desert. Our Saviour is not limited to a special place. Wherever a longing soul cries to Him for help he will find Him. "Then shalt thou call, and the Lord shall answer; thou shalt cry, and he shall say, *Here I am*" (Isa. 58: 9).

The incense on the altar of incense was lit from the fire on the altar of burnt-offering. God punished Nadab and Abihu for offering strange fire on the altar. Our worship should be not of self-will, but in harmony with our God. The same time the lamb was offered on the altar of burnt-offering, the incense rose from the altar of incense.

No animal was to be offered on the altar in the holy place. "For *by one offering*, he hath perfected for ever them that are sanctified" (Heb. 10: 14).

The Lord had Himself ordered the sweet spices, stacte, and onyche, and galbanum in equal parts. To these sweet spices should be added frankincense. Scofield points out that we are told the component parts of the incense, but Scripture does not tell us the component parts of frankincense, and he suggests that where all point to the perfections of Christ, which we may to some extent apprehend the balm which the Good Samaritan applies to our wounds, the sweet sympathy which makes Him feel with us in our sufferings; the frankincense is the excellencies which the Father sees in His Son and through which our prayers are accepted in the beloved. This sweet perfume was only to be made for the service in the holies and it was not to be used for ordinary purposes. It was to be holy unto the Lord. If any Israelite should use it for common purpose, he was to be cut off from the people.

"Lord, I cry unto thee: make haste unto me; give ear unto my voice, when I cry unto thee. Let my prayer be set *forth before thee as incense*; and the lifting up of my hands as *the evening sacrifice*" (Ps. 141: 1, 2). When the morning and evening sacrifice was brought to the Lord in the court, the priest took of the fire and in the inner sanctuary lit the incense on the altar. Prayer and incense are closely connected. "The four and twenty elders fell down before the Lamb, having every one of them harps, and *golden vials full of odours,* which are the prayers of the saints" (Rev. 5: 8).

There is not enough worship in many of our prayers; the incense is wanting. Our Lord told the Samaritan woman that the Lord seeks *worshippers* that worship Him in spirit and in truth (John 4: 23). Andrew Murray in his most helpful book, *With Christ in the School of Prayer,* points out that Christ mentioned three classes of worshippers: (1) The Samaritans who worshipped what they did not know; (2) The Jews who had the true knowledge of God; (3) We worship that *which we know;* for salvation is of the Jews. But the hour had come when the real worshippers would worship God in *spirit and in truth.* This means more than to pray earnestly. Many of the believing Jews did that and no doubt also some of the Samaritans. God is a Spirit and there must be harmony between God and His worshippers. "Like seeks like" is a law of Nature and is also a law in the spiritual world. There must be kinship; it is the child that speaks to Father. Spiritual worship is only possible through the indwelling Holy Spirit filling the heart of the believer. There are still many who like the Samaritans pray without knowing; they approach the Lord with their lips, their heart is far from them. To many of God's children James would say: "Ye have not because ye ask not." Oh, for a spirit of prayer and supplication to be poured upon God's people in these ominous times! Christ still says: "The Father seeks worshippers that worship him in Spirit and in truth."

The incense was composed of four precious spices: stacte and onycha, galbanum and pure frankincense. These sweet spices should not fail in the prayers of

God's people: *Worship, Prayer, Supplication and Thanksgiving.*

The Father seeks worshippers (John 4: 23). Our Lord taught us to pray to our Father, but He added "Which is in heaven." We approach Him who dwelleth in eternity whose name is holy; we are in the audience chamber of the King of kings, the Lord of lords. Surely then it beseems us to come to Him in reverence and godly fear. How precious are those moments of silence in concentration as we meditate on Him to whom we are going to speak, and reflect on what we shall bring before Him. "O God, open then my lips and my mouth shall show forth thy praise." Abraham said: "Behold now, I have taken upon me to speak unto the Lord, which am but dust and ashes" (Gen. 18: 27). Let us lift up our hearts. Let us meditate on that infinite love of our heavenly Father, as He has revealed it in our Lord Jesus Christ, in the mercy and goodness which have followed us all the days of our life, and our hearts will be filled with gratitude, praise and *worship.*

Our Lord in answer to the request of His disciples gave them that wonderful prayer so simple that a child can pray it, so deep that it contains our innermost longings. The Lord's prayer, because He gave it to us; the disciples' prayer, because He intended if for our use. How He puts our heavenly Father's interests before our own! How He teaches us first to say: Thy name, Thy kingdom, Thy will before we ask *give us, lead us, deliver us.* Blessed Lord, teach me how to pray, that *Thy* honour, *Thy* Kingdom should have the pre-eminence in my thought and prayer-life.

Intercession will certainly then have a large space in our prayer-life. We shall ask the Lord to lay some souls on our hearts for whose salvation we have to pray. A young man was lying months on a sick-bed. He was in the last stage of consumption. After his home-call his mother found a paper with the names of more than twenty of his friends who he had successively prayed into the kingdom. Personally, I never had a doubt that the Lord would hear my prayers for my children because I felt sure it was a prayer in harmony with the will of God (1 John 5: 14).

I met one of my young friends this morning. He had just come from a quiet time with his Lord. I asked him to show me a little book he had in his hand. He had divided the different mission fields in which he was interested and the missionaries he had met over the days of the month. Asia, Africa, China, India, Europe, South America had a place in it. I asked him to put my name in it. I owe a great deal in my service to faithful prayer-partners, and I am quite sure many in Africa, India, China and South America have received also new courage, a new inspiration, and vision by the faithful prayers of their prayer-partners at home. The greatest missionary that ever lived, Saint Paul, needed the prayers of the churches which he had been able to found. He appealed to the Roman church in this touching way: "Now I *beseech* you, brethren, for *the Lord Jesus Christ's sake*, and for the love of the Spirit, that ye *strive together with me* in your prayers to God for me" (Rom. 15: 30). If Saint Paul felt the need of their prayers, do you not think we, his humble successors, stand in far greater need of them? Do you think you have any right to send out missionaries unless you support them by your prayers in their work for the Master, in their moments of loneliness, weariness, weakness and temptation?

Beloved, we are standing at the altar of incense. Do you see the One who is standing beside it? It is our faithful high priest who ever liveth to make intercession for us (Heb. 7 : 25). He continues to pray for us, as He did for His disciples on earth. It is to His intercession that our prayers are acceptable in the beloved. His incense is added to the prayers of His saints. As we share His life, shall we not also share His work? Shall we not be in fellowship with Him in His work of intercession?

I should be so thankful if this study would lead some of my readers to start a prayer-list. In that case, may I advise you before you close your list to do what the Lord tells us in Matthew 5 : 44. If you do this you will soon discover a double result, not only objective, but subjective as well. Prayer will change our disposition to people who have been unkind to us.

Pray "for kings and all that are in authority" (1 Tim. 2 : 2). How often I have listened to criticisms of those in authority; how seldom I have heard God's children pray for them. How people on whose shoulders rest such tremendous responsibilities need our prayers!

Thanksgiving is one of the sweet spices that should not fail in our prayers. How much we have to thank the Lord for, how many answers to prayers! How often I have prayed with a happy young mother (Ps. 116). "I will offer to thee the sacrifice of thanksgiving and will call upon the name of the Lord" (Ps. 116: 17).

"*Ask* and it shall be given you; *seek*, and ye shall find, *knock*, and it shall be opened unto you" (Matt. 7: 7). That is the law in the kingdom. Begin with asking; soon you will want not only gifts but will long for the Giver. You will seek and find. Then you will always want Him to be with you; you will want the indwelling Christ. He will come up and sup with you and you with Him.

Pray for your friends! The Lord turned Job's captivity when he prayed for his friends (Job 42: 10). He will do the same to you. Accustom yourself to talk with the Lord about everything. The Queen of Sheba communed with Solomon all that was in her heart (1 Kings 10: 3). "She told him all her plans," according to another version. You will be wise if you do the same. It may save you many a false step. If the Master does not approve of your plans, then you drop them. Tell Him about all your difficulties. He will find a way out. If anybody has been unkind to you, tell Him. He will help you bear it. Tell Him about your work, about the visits you have paid, the letters you have received or written, about the book you have been reading. It all concerns Him. And if you tell Him about your sorrows, do not forget to tell Him about your joys. Let Him share your life. Make it a habit to consult Him and talk with Him about everything; anxiety, and worry will flee. Our Lord is a good listener and He always has time for you. Do not forget to give Him a chance to talk to you too. Remember, prayer is a dialogue, not a monologue; and what He says to you is more important that what you say to Him.

Our Lord spent much time in prayer: When He commenced His public ministry (Luke 3: 21); when He chose His apostles (Luke 6: 12); when on the mount of transfiguration (Luke 9: 29); after a hard day's work when His disciples were struggling with the waves, He was on the mount praying. If our Lord felt the need of prayer, do we not need it much more?

May I ask you a question? How much time do you spend each day in prayer? Have you been at the altar of incense today? Daniel prayed three times a day. Business of state took so much of his time, the responsibility resting on his shoulders was so great, that he felt the need of a breathing-space in the middle of the day. The span of time between morning and evening prayers was too large. He built a bridge. Do the same. It will give you balance, peace and concentration of mind. It will help you to grow in grace.

We have been meditating at the altar of incense. We have recognized that we do not pray enough; that our prayer life is the thermometer of our inner life. We have seen how our Father-God is waiting to bestow His gifts on us. He only waits for our asking. It is like us to think of ourselves and the benefits we receive through prayer. Have you ever thought of the fact that you are Father's child and that He longs to see you and hear your voice? I am a father. I have been away from home now nearly two years. Do you know that I am often homesick for a sight of my children? I know a mother who every Monday waited for a letter from her boy in another country; who, a fortnight before he came home for his vacation, made his room ready for him. I know that when the day drew near she counted the hours before the train arrived at the little country station, and wondered whether the steamer had been delayed. I have dear children now myself; they love their father, but I feel sure Father longs more for a sight of His children than the child looks for the father. Father loves you; how much I cannot tell you. He gave His best for you, and He loves to see His child. He says: "Seek ye my face!" Let the response of my heart be: "Thy face, Lord, will I seek" (Ps. 27: 8).

The Ark of the Testimony

22

THE ARK OF THE TESTIMONY AND THE MERCY SEAT

10. And they shall make an ark of acacia wood:
two cubits and a half shall be the length thereof,
and a cubit and a half the breadth thereof, and a
cubit and a half the height thereof.

11. And thou shalt overlay it with pure gold,
within and without shalt thou overlay it, and shalt
make upon it a crown of gold round about.

17. And thou shalt make a mercy seat of pure
gold: two cubits and a half shall be the length
thereof, and a cubit and a half the breadth thereof.

21. And thou shalt put the mercy seat above upon
the ark; and in the ark thou shalt put the testimony
that I shall give thee.—EXODUS 25: 10, 11, 17, 21

How the hearts of the children of Israel must have
been full of holy joy and gratitude when God made
them the gracious promise that He would dwell amongst
them! How gladly they brought their offerings to make
a sanctuary for the Most High! God Himself had shown
Moses on the mount the pattern, and they were to make
it *even* as it had been shown to Moses (Exod. 25: 9).
God has a plan for each of His children, for their lives
and service. He can only be responsible for *His plan.*
Often we make our own plans and incur responsibilities which God does not want us to take with its re-
sultant cares and anxieties. He tells us in His Word
that we ought to love and walk and give as our Lord

201

walked and loved and gave. God has a plan for your future; He planned the work you should do; and, in fact, I believe for every day and hour of your life. He shows it to you through the Holy Spirit and also through the trend of circumstances. Let us work according to the pattern.

The five chapters, Exodus 25–30, describing the tabernacle and its contents, fall into two divisions. God begins with showing us the ark of the testimony and the mercy seat, and then leads through the holy place by the golden candlestick shedding its light on the table of shewbread and the altar of incense, through the vail, past the brazen laver to the altar of burnt-offering. In chapters 25–7: 19 we trace the way which God takes to meet man. In God's ways of salvation, described all through the Bible from the very beginning, where God meets fallen man with the question: "Adam, where art thou?" it is God that stoops down to meet man, not man going to meet God. Our Lord Jesus Christ travelled all the way from the mercy seat to the altar of burnt-offering. "For the joy set before him, he endured the cross, and despised the shame, and then went the way back to the throne" (Heb. 12: 2). Open the gates wide, that the King of Glory may come in.

"Blessed is he whose transgression is forgiven, whose sin is covered" (Ps. 32: 1). Every Israelite who had entered the gate of the court and at the brazen altar had confessed his sin and had laid his hand on the animal that was to die in his stead, could say that. Reader, are your sins covered by the blood of Christ? Have you entered the gate of the court? There is only one door. Jesus is the door.

Saved to serve. "What shall I render unto the Lord for all his benefits toward me?" (Ps. 116: 12). He longs to serve his Lord, to consecrate his life to his Lord's service, to enter the sanctuary. Only priests are allowed to enter. He that hath loved us and washed us from our sins with His own blood has made us kings and priests to God our Father. Once more, therefore, he approaches the altar of burnt-offering, not this time with a sin-offering. That has been burnt outside the camp. His sins have been covered, so this time he brings a burnt-offering which has to be consumed on the altar as an offering of sweet odour unto the Lord. Now with clean hands and feet the priest may enter the holy place. Enlightened by the Holy Ghost, he may feed on the Word and lead a life of prayer and service.

Many of God's children stop at the brazen altar. They have accepted the Lord as their Saviour, but have remained in the court. They have never heeded the call of the Master: "Go ye also and work in my vineyard." They have never become soul-winners. A soul saved; a life lost for the Master. I pray that every reader may dedicate his life to the service of the Lord and not stand before Him empty-handed. The time may be short in which we have the privilege of winning souls. "The night cometh when no man can work."

Under the old covenant, only the high priest was allowed once a year on the day of atonement to enter the Holiest of all, and not without blood. Now the vail has been rent in twain. Christ has opened for us a new and living way through His own broken heart, and with boldness we may now approach the throne of grace, to find grace to help in time of need.

"Make an ark of acacia wood, . . . overlay it with pure gold, within and without, . . . make staves of acacia wood, and overlay them with gold. . . . The staves shall be in the rings of the ark: they shall not be taken from it" (Exod. 25: 10–15).

In the Holiest was only one object, consisting of two parts: the lower part was called the ark of testimony; the upper part was the mercy seat. The ark was of acacia wood overlaid with gold within and without, pointing to the human and divine natures of our blessed Lord. Two staves overlaid with gold were put through the four golden rings and were not to be taken out of them. The priests had to carry it on their shoulders before the Israelites when the cloud by day or the fiery pillar by night rose.

"The ark of the covenant of the Lord went before them to *search out a resting-place* for them" (Num. 10: 33). Oh, the loving-kindness and care of the Lord for His people! Wherever the people were, the Lord was. He never left nor forsook them. For instance, there was a time when it was hard to secure a suitable home. They were scarce. How many of God's children have proved at that time that our Father-God is the best Real-Estate man and provides for His children. "He shall choose our inheritance for us" (Ps. 47: 4). The good Shepherd still goes before His sheep. Lord, help us to follow Thee closely!

As long as the children of Israel journeyed in the wilderness, the ark went before them. When they had settled in the promised land and the temple of Solomon was built, the staves were taken out of the ark.

In the ark were the two tables of stone on which God

had written the Ten Commandments. When, in our meditation, we look at that ark in the Holiest, we lift up our hearts to the Lord Jesus, of which the ark of testimony was such a wonderful type, to him who said: "I delight to do thy will, O my God: yea, thy law is within my heart" (Ps. 40: 8).

Once before God had given to Moses two tables on which He Himself had written the commandments. As Moses went down the mount he saw how the children of Israel worshipped the golden calf and, angry at the idolatry of his people, he cast the tables out of his hand and broke them (Exod. 32: 19). God commanded Moses to bring two new tables and once more wrote the commandments upon them. These were the tables that God commanded Moses to lay up in the ark of the testimony. These unbroken tables are *a type of the perfect obedience of our Lord.* "He was not rebellious, neither turned away back" (Isa. 50: 5). "He was obedient unto death, even the death on the cross" (Phil. 2: 8). Moses can only show us broken tablets through which we can never be saved. Jesus and Jesus alone is the true ark of testimony, where righteousness and peace kissed each other (Ps. 85: 10), the mediator between God and a fallen race. *"Christ is the end of the law* for righteousness to every one that believeth" (Rom. 10: 4).

An ark without the mercy seat would not have afforded a refuge to a sinful race. God is holy and merciful, but He is also just. The law of Moses, the stone tablets, had been broken. "Whosoever shall keep the whole law, and yet offend in one point, he is guilty of all" (James 2: 10). Israel had not sinned against one commandment, but against all. So have we. How terrible an ark without a mercy seat: an uncovered law, a silent witness against each one of us! An open ark is a seat of justice, not a seat of mercy.

"Thou shalt make a mercy seat of pure gold" (Exod. 25: 17). The mercy seat was the cover of the ark. On both ends was a cherub, their eyes looking at the mercy seat, as if anxious to fathom that great mystery of godliness: *"God was manifest in the flesh"* (1 Tim. 3: 16).

The mercy seat must cover the whole ark. Nothing could be seen of the two tables. Jesus covered the commandments. Our own righteousness is as filthy rags; they cannot cover us. The mercy seat had to have the same length and breadth as the ark. The mercy seat must be pure and flawless. The eye of the Holy One must be able to rest on it with pleasure. Therefore, it had to be made of pure gold.

The mercy seat must be sprinkled with blood. Each year on the day of atonement, the high priest entered the Holiest to sprinkle the mercy seat. Otherwise it would not have been a shelter for a fallen race.

Mercy seat, what message hast thou for a sinner seeking pardon and grace? The Holy Spirit gives us the answer: "Being justified freely by his grace through the redemption that is in Christ Jesus: whom God hath set forth to be a propitiation through faith in his blood" (Rom. 3: 24, 25).

Jesus Christ is our mercy seat. His righteousness is not too short, it covers all our sin. His blood cleanses us from all sin. There is power in the blood to set us free from all sinful habits. Reader, have you ever been to the mercy seat? It is the only place where you can be reconciled with God. Your blameless life, your unselfish character, your kind deeds cannot save you. If you trust in your merits, your house is built on shifting sand. You will find no mercy there. Mercy you can only find at the mercy seat. You can go there now. You need no priest, no man to open the way for you. The vail has been rent in twain. The way is open. Do not delay. You do not know whether you can still come tomorrow.

"Let us therefore come boldly to the throne of grace, that we may obtain mercy, and find grace to help in time of need" (Heb. 4: 16).

LOVE'S HIGHWAY
From the depths of the doom and darkness
  Ascends that wondrous road
Which leads from the heart of the sinner
  Up to the heart of God.
For from heights of the golden City,
  God made the glorious road
Which leads to the sinner
  Down from the heart of God.
        —*From manuscript of the earlier part
        of the fourteenth century.*

23

A POT OF MANNA AND A BUDDING ROD

> And Moses said unto Aaron, Take a pot, and put *an omer full of manna* therein, and lay it up before the Lord, *to be kept for your generations.*—EXODUS 16:33
>
> 8. On the morrow Moses went into the tabernacle of witness; and, behold, *the rod of Aaron* for the house of Levi *was budded, and brought forth buds,* and *bloomed blossoms,* and *yielded almonds.*
>
> 10. And the Lord said unto Moses, Bring Aaron's rod again before the testimony, to be kept for a token against the rebels; and thou shalt take away their murmurings from me, that they die not.
> —NUMBERS 17: 8, 10

Two memorials, one of human folly and sin, and one of divine mercy and grace, God commanded Moses to put into the ark.

God had done mighty deeds for Israel. He had delivered them out of the hand of their Egyptian taskmasters. He had led them safely through the Red Sea. He had made the bitter water of Mara sweet. He had been a shelter from the heat for them in providing the palm-trees of Elim, and notwithstanding His loving care, they soon began to murmur against Him that He had only led them in the dreary desert to starve them by hunger and thirst. It seems all but incredible to us when we read this of others.

In response to this want of confidence, God provided them each day with fresh food from heaven during the forty years of their wanderings in the desert. "He hath not dealt with us after our sins; neither rewarded us according to our iniquities" (Ps. 103: 10). Of this manna, angels' food for His children, God commanded that an omer, a man's daily portion, should be put into the ark in a little pot to be kept for generations. Some Israelites tried to keep manna for the next day; it became bad; it bred worms. We cannot live on past blessings. The only way to deal with them is to pass them on to others. What we commit unto the Lord, He is able to keep till the great day. The manna in the ark did not turn bad.

That *they may see the bread* with which I have fed you in the wilderness. We are so apt to forget. Our memory is also perverted by sin. We forget what we should remember and we remember things we should forget. David says: "Bless the Lord, O my soul, and *forget not all his benefits.*" David thought we were most likely to forget most of them. "Count your many blessings, count them one by one, and it will surprise you what the Lord has done." The Lord knows our frame. We need the pot of omer filled with manna; we need the *Holy Spirit, the best Remembrancer.* What is manna? An Israelite would have answered: "It is a small round thing; it looks like corriander seed; it is sweet to the taste and so light that it fell on the dew in early morning."

Our Lord answered: "My Father giveth you the true bread from heaven. I am the bread of life: he that cometh to me shall never hunger; and he that believeth on me shall never thirst" (John 6: 32, 36).

How is it that many of God's children look starved?

Father is not to blame. In Father's house is bread enough and to spare (Luke 15:17). The fault lies with the children. Healthy children have a good appetite. They do not forget their meals. They like home-food best. Sick children have no healthy appetite. Some of the Israelites were sick. They longed for the flesh-pots of Egypt because their heart was still in Egypt. My friend, you cannot live on the blessings you received yesterday; you must gather fresh manna every morning when your mind is fresh, before you open your post or your newspaper.

Your soul gets starved if you spend more time on your newspaper and magazines than on the Word of God. Read the Bible with your children; read it for yourself and you will grow in grace and in the knowledge of Jesus Christ. The more you study the Bible, the more you will love it. Dig deep and you will discover the hidden treasures of darkness (Isa. 45:3). You will not complain about the drought, for "the Lord shall *guide* thee *continually*, and *satisfy* thy *soul* in *drought*, and make fat thy bones: and thou shalt be like a *watered garden*, and like a spring of water, whose waters fail not" (Isa. 58:11).

Besides the pot of manna, a token of God's loving care for His people, a type of our Lord Jesus Christ, the true bread of life, there was Aaron's rod, a sign of Israel's murmuring and disobedience. If that rod could speak, what a sad story it would have to tell! Korah, Dathan and Abiram wanted to be great. The sixteenth chapter of Numbers is one of the saddest in the whole Bible. Korah and his two friends were dissatisfied. They rebelled against Moses and Aaron. They envied them the place to which God had called them. The poison of dissatisfaction and rebellion had spread amongst the chief princes and the people. The Pharisees sought the first places in the synagogue. Christ says: "He who will be first among you, let him be the servant of all." God laid His hand in punishment on Korah, Dathan and Abiram. They had provoked the Lord. The earth swallowed them up and they perished from among the congregation (Num. 16: 33).

Had this dreadful punishment brought Israel in repentance on their knees? We might have expected so. Instead, the next morning they reproached Aaron again for having assumed a position to which he had no right. I am so glad that in the whole story there is not a word of defence on the part of Aaron. He had committed his cause to the Lord and He would legitimate His servants. We too have an advocate with the Father, and if we commit our cause to Him, there is no necessity of defending ourselves (1 John 2: 1). How much time and anxiety this saves us. *The Lord shall fight you, and ye shall hold your peace"* (Exod. 14: 14).

"Commit thy way unto the Lord; trust also in him; and *he starts doing"* (Ps. 37: 5). He always does even if we fail to notice it. He sometimes has to keep us waiting and keeps away encouraging results until we learn to trust the Lord without them, and then the result will be all the more wonderful. The Lord commanded that the head of each tribe should bring his rod and put his name on it. Aaron represented the tribe of Levi, chosen by God to minister in the tabernacle for the people. Moses put the twelve rods before the Lord before the ark of witness. God said that "the man's rod whom *I shall choose*, shall blossom: and I will make to cease from me the murmurings of the children of Israel." The next morning Moses went into the tabernacle and behold the rod of Aaron was budded, *brought forth buds*, and *bloomed blossoms*, and yielded almonds (Num. 17: 8). The buds of spring, the green leaves of early summer, the fruit of autumn—God had done a miracle and legitimated His servant who had entrusted his case to Him.

Was Aaron's rod so much better than the others? No, it was not. God had worked a miracle: He still does. Aaron's rod speaks to us of want and fullness. In the evening Aaron's rod differed in no respect from those of the other princes. There was no life whatever in it; it was a dead stick. If you had asked anybody they would have said: "It is quite impossible that that stick could ever blossom." It did not bear fruit either. Where there is no life, there is no fruitfulness. Fruit is the result of the juice which, from the roots, flows through the branches.

Aaron's rod was not only dead, but fruitless. It had no value. The carpenter could make nothing out of it. "What is the vine-tree more than any other tree? Shall wood be taken thereof?" the prophet asks. As a living branch of the vine it can bear fruit, more fruit, much fruit. Apart from the vine it can do nothing. You cannot even hang something on it. The carpenter can make use of other wood, but branches of the vine are only good for firewood (Ezek. 15: 2–4).

Now look at that same rod the next morning. If Aaron's name had not been carved into it, you would not have recognized it. It was a new creation. It budded, and brought forth buds, and bloomed blossoms, and yielded almonds. Fresh life is sprouted out everywhere. The blooms spread a lovely odour all around. The rod, instead of being repulsive, attracts people. When the Christ-life manifests itself in us, we find grace by God and man. We are a sweet odour of Christ. If you have spent a day in the tulip fields of Holland you smell of the tulip fields. If you have been with Christ long enough, it will make people think of Christ when they meet you. You are *a sweet savour of Christ* (2 Cor. 2: 15), an epistle of Christ, a recommendation of Christ, written not with ink, but *with the Spirit* of the *living God,* commending Christ to your surroundings. You are "like a tree planted by the rivers of water, that bringeth forth his fruit in his season; his leaf also shall not wither; and whatsoever he doeth shall prosper" (Ps. 1: 3). Is this really possible? A wonder must happen. You are right, but we reckon with a Saviour whose name is *"Wonderful,"* who can restore *the years that the locust has eaten* and who *will do great things* (Joel 2: 25).

24

THE ARK OF TESTIMONY GUIDING THE PEOPLE

My presence shall go with thee, and I will give thee
rest.—EXODUS 33: 44

BEFORE closing our studies on the ark, let us follow
for a few moments the story of the ark. Moses had
prayed: "If thy presence go not with me, carry us not
up hence" (Exod. 33: 15). The Lord graciously heard
the prayer of His servant: "My presence shall go with
thee and I will give thee rest" (Exod. 33: 14). As proof
that the prayer was heard, God gave His people the ark
of the covenant. It was a visible sign of the invisible
presence of God.

In vain Moses had tried to induce his brother-in-law,
Hobab, to be their guide during their wanderings in
the wilderness. God did better for Moses. The ark of
the covenant of the Lord went before them in a three-
days' journey to search out a resting-place for them
(Num. 10: 33). To many young missionaries going out
to the mission field, I have passed on the promise: "I
will go before thee, and make the crooked places
straight: I will break in pieces the gates of brass, and
cut in sunder the bars of iron" (Isa. 45: 2). How often
have I tried with my puny hands to break in sunder
iron gates. I did only achieve to hurt my own hands.
He gives *an open door* to people that *have little strength*

(Rev. 3: 8). He never expects the impossible from us, and as the ark went before the children of Israel, so the good Shepherd goes before His sheep (John 10: 4), and the best bits of food are for the sheep that keep closest to His side.

The Jordan separated the children of Israel from the promised land of Canaan. It was harvest time and the Jordan overflowed all the banks. Of course, that was no hindrance to God. The Israelites had to go to the banks of the river. God did the rest. As soon as the feet of the priests dipped in the brim of the water, God made the waters stand that came from above, and those that flowed into the Dead Sea stopped (Joshua 3: 16). The priests with the ark stood in the midst of Jordan till all Israel had passed *clean over Jordan.* Not the holiness of the children of Israel, but God's presence kept the waters back. Have you gone *clean over Jordan?* You will never enter the land of rest unless you do. Are you buried with Christ? (Rom. 6: 6–11). God's children have looked up to the cross. There is life in a look to the crucified one.

Let us not only look up at the cross, but look down at it from God's standpoint. He sees on that cross not only His Son dying for us, but also all the redeemed through His precious blood, crucified with Him. *"Reckon yourself dead with Christ"* (Rom. 6: 11). God will make your reckoning true. Go clean over Jordan. Leave Egypt and the wilderness behind you and enter the Promised Land.

The host of Israel camped before Jericho. Its high walls had to fall before they could enter Canaan. It barred the way to a life of victory. No one could go in or out (Joshua 6: 1). Jesus has the keys also of your Jericho (Rev. 3: 7). The ark of the covenant went round about Jericho—the high walls fell down. The presence of Jesus brings victory (Phil. 3: 21).

When there is a ban among us God cannot give us victory. Achan had taken of the accursed spoils of Jericho and the host of Israel suffered defeat. Then Joshua and the elders of Israel fell upon their faces *before the ark* from morning till evening. God showed them the transgressor and his sin. The ban was removed and God gave again victory.

The Philistines had defeated Israel. The elders suggested that the ark should be fetched from Shiloh. The Israelites shouted with joy when Eli's sons, Hophni and Phinehas, brought the ark. They thought the ark would be sure to bring them victory. Instead, they suffered a worse defeat and the ark fell into the hands of the Philistines (1 Sam. 4: 11). Was God not present? God stood in the midst of an unholy people and therefore He could not fight for them. "I will *go and return to my place, till they acknowledge their offence, and seek my face*: in their affliction they will seek me early." (Hos. 5: 15). That is a solemn word also for our times.

The Philistines took the ark and put it into the house of their idol (1 Sam. 5: 1–2). Where God is, there is no room for idols. Our God is a jealous God. He wants whole-hearted devotion. They found Dagon fallen on his face. The Philistines experienced what it means to have a holy God in their midst. God's presence was for them a savour of death unto death (2 Cor. 2: 16). In those seven months that the ark was with the Philistines, God had made it plain to them that He is a holy

God and they sought as soon as possible to get rid of Him. The Philistines sought the advice of their wise men and they suggested that a new cart should be made and the ark and trespass-offering put on it. Two milch kine should be yoked to it who had never drawn a cart before and their calves kept away from them. If these milch kine should not take the road to Israel, all the disasters which had befallen them were only due to chance, but if they went towards Beth-shemesh the hand of Israel's God had been hard upon them; and the kine went towards Beth-shemesh followed by the Philistine princes.

The ark was received with shouts of joy. In frivolous curiosity the inhabitants opened the ark to look at its contents. God is not a respecter of persons. That day fifty thousand and seventy men of Israel fell (1 Sam. 6: 19).

God was too holy for the inhabitants of Beth-shemesh. They asked the inhabitants of Kirjath-jearim to take the ark. They consented and fetched the ark and brought it to the house of Abinadab. Twenty long years the ark of the Lord was in the little town on the borderland. How long has the Lord been waiting at your door for you to welcome Him as your King? "Behold, I stand at the door and knock" (Rev. 3: 20). These words were not spoken to the unconverted, but to a church, the church of Laodicea. It took God seven months to subdue the Philistines, but twenty years had to pass before Israel yielded to their God.

God had chosen David to be king of Israel. He had to go through a hard training school before the Lord put him on the throne. David became a man of faith, trusting the Lord. The Lord gave him victory over his enemies. David wanted to give the Lord the first place in his kingdom. The ark of the covenant should no longer dwell in the borderland. With a guard of honour of thirty thousand men David fetched the ark from Kirjath-jearim. It should be a day of national rejoicing. It became a day of mourning.

David had ordered a new cart for the ark. Uzzah and Ahio, the sons of Abinadab, were to drive it. No doubt David meant well. He wanted to honour the ark of the covenant. God had decreed that the ark should be borne on the living shoulders of consecrated men. Obedience is better than sacrifice. We love new carts. We make new birthday carts full of good resolutions and place the ark on it. We drive instead of being driven; conducting instead of being constrained; imposing our human thoughts on God's thoughts, whereas His thoughts are higher than ours. God looks to His children for obedience, simple obedience, not new carts. Obedience is better than sacrifice. There are new carts in our churches in the present time.

The oxen shook the cart and Uzzah stretched out his hand to steady it. No doubt Uzzah meant well. With the best of intentions, and yet presumptive, he stretched out his hand to steady the ark, but the hand dropped, it was a lifeless hand. We too are often inclined to stretch out the hand to steady the ark. It often seems to me that God gave David the thirty-seventh Psalm especially for our times. "Rest in the Lord and wait patiently for him: fret not thyself" (Ps. 37 : 7). God wants rested workers. Keep in harmony with the will of God. "Commit thy way unto the Lord, trust also in him, and he starts doing" (Ps. 37:5). How we need to learn the art of committing and trusting Father. Those who trust Him fully find Him wholly true. "Thou wilt keep him in *perfect peace*, whose mind is stayed on thee: *because he trusteth in thee*" (Isa. 26:3). When we live the life of faith we commit ourselves, our future to Him, leaving things alone, keeping our hands off. Resting in the Lord, we trust all will be well even when all seems to go wrong.

God smote Uzzah for his error and there he died. That day was not a day of rejoicing. David was displeased, I hope, with himself. He acknowledged how unworthy he was to receive the ark in the city of David, and carried it into the house of Obed-Edom, where it rested for three months. The Lord blessed the house of Obed-Edom because of the ark. "If a man love me, he will keep my words: and my Father will love him, and we will come unto him, and make our abode with him" (John 14:23).

David heard this good news and it encouraged him to have the ark brought to Jerusalem, for he too wanted a blessing for him and his house. This time David had not a new cart made. "David said, None ought to carry the ark of God but the Levites: for them hath the Lord chosen to carry the ark of God, and to minister unto him forever" (1 Chron. 15:2). David had learned his lesson. The way of obedience is always a way of blessing. With great joy the ark was placed in the midst of the tabernacle which David had pitched for it (2 Sam. 6:17).

The servant of the Lord, David's greatest desire was to build a house for the Lord. His wish, like Moses', was not granted. David's hands were stained with blood. God promised him, however, that after he had been called home his son Solomon should build the temple. David acknowledged the righteousness and mercy of God's decree. He had the happy privilege to collect all the treasures needed for the building of the temple. When it was finished, *"the priests brought the ark of the covenant* of the Lord *unto his place, into the most holy place,* even under the wings of the cherubim" (2 Chron. 5: 7).

The ark remained in the temple till Nebuchadnezzar, king of Babylon, conquered Jerusalem and led the Jews into captivity in Babylon. The temple was burned down and with it its costly vessels and, no doubt, also the ark became a prey of the flames.

Tradition says that in the second temple a large stone was placed on the spot where the ark had stood, that the ark was buried under the temple and will be found again when the new temple will be built.

God's children look forward to a different future. They look forward to the coming of their Lord, meeting the Lord in the air, being together with the Lord and with their dear ones who have gone before (1 Thess. 4: 16–20). They look forward to the time when our Lord's feet will stand on the mount of Olives (Zech. 14: 4); when God will pour out the spirit of supplication and prayer on His people, Israel; when they will see Him who they have pierced; when the great battle of Armageddon will be fought and the Lord will come to the rescue of His people (Zech. 12: 10); when Jesus Christ will reign victorious and all the earth shall own His sway; when swords shall be beaten into ploughshares and spears into pruning hooks; when nation shall not lift up sword against nation, neither shall they learn war any more (Isa. 2: 4). Then we shall want neither ark nor temple, but Jesus Christ will be our King for ever and ever.

"Peace I leave with you, my peace I give unto you" (John 14: 27) is one of the most precious promises of our Saviour. Peace He left us when He suffered for us and died for us on the cross. The peace He gives us comes into our heart through a living fellowship with our high priest in glory. It is a peace like a river, inexhaustible, it is Jesus-peace. Even amongst the severest trials and afflictions, that undisturbed peace was His; "semper idem," He was always the same.

The voice of Jesus whispers:

> Peace, perfect peace in this dark world of sin?
> The voice of Jesus whispers: "Peace within!"

This deep inward peace is the happy part of God's children who live in the Holiest of holies. I am not at all surprised that an old Scotch shepherd, being asked on his sick-bed if he was going to heaven, answered: "Brother, I have been living there for the last ten years." There are wilderness-Christians and Canaan-Christians. The old man lived in Canaan. Jesus has come not only that we might have life, but have it more *abundantly* (John 10: 10). Genesis 1: 26 shows us a transformation in His image and likeness.

Our first step was the entrance through the gate into the court. I trust each of my readers has taken that step. The altar of burnt-offerings speaks of a whole-hearted consecration and full surrender. The laver of daily cleansing, the golden candlestick of the fullness of the Holy Spirit; the table of shewbread of fullness of power of joy and peace; the altar of incense of a daily life of prayer in partnership with our High Priest. Reader, do you know all these precious gifts of a loving Father through His Son and Spirit by happy experience?

There remains only one step more to take and God only knows when that step will be taken. It is the last step here on earth and leads into Father's mansion with the many rooms.

The tabernacle speaks of a life on earth, the temple of Solomon of a life in glory. The pot of manna and Aaron's blooming rod are no longer in the tabernacle. There nothing will remind us of our murmuring and ingratitude.

There was a time when I believed we could only enter into Canaan through the valley of the shadow of death. Now I know that here already we can enter into that rest. Reader, if you have followed me through the court into the sanctuary and into the Holiest of holies you have made that happy experience.

Some time ago we read in our family worship that wonderful first page of the Bible. It shows us seven steps. It begins with God. It finishes with God. He is the beginning and the end. It speaks of emptiness and darkness; how empty the heart is without Jesus. We see how the Holy Spirit gives *light* in the dark soul and *illumines* it. In the seventh verse we find division and separation as a second step. At the altar of burnt-offering we leave everything that would not please the Master. The laver cleanses feet and hands from daily coming in contact with sinful earth. Genesis 1: 7 speaks not only of growth but fruitfulness. Genesis 1: 7 shows us that heaven rules the earth and that we have taken Jesus not only as our Saviour but crowned Him as King. Genesis 1: 22 speaks of life abundant—Jesus. All our sins are blotted out. God has cast them behind in the depths of the sea of His unfathomable love. All our sorrows will be forgotten, there is no night, only day— eternal day. "The lamb is the light thereof." "Now we see through a glass darkly; but then face to face : now I know in part; but then shall I know even as also I am known. And now abideth faith, hope, love, these three; but the greatest of these is love."

> And I shall see Him face to face
> And tell the story: Saved by grace.

Other Books on the Tabernacle

**DEVOTIONAL OUTLINES
ON THE TABERNACLE**   **Glenn M. Jones.**
In this systematic introduction to the great theme and purpose of the tabernacle, the reader will see the Lord Jesus Christ through the beauty, craft, materials, colors, furniture and sacrifices of this unique center of worship. Excellent for group Bible study.
ISBN 0-8254-2966-8   80 pp.   paper

OUTLINE STUDIES OF THE TABERNACLE   **Ada R. Habershon**
A thought-provoking outline study on the construction, erection and service of the tabernacle.
ISBN 0-8254-2820-3   64 pp.   paper

TABERNACLE IN THE WILDERNESS   **John Ritchie**
A concise, practical study of the tabernacle, the offerings and the priesthood which all typify the person and work of Christ. A thrilling parallel between the Old Testament tabernacle and a Christian's daily walk is presented. Illustrated.
ISBN 0-8254-3616-8   120 pp.   paper

THOUGHTS ON THE TABERNACLE   **J. Denham Smith**
Beautiful, devotional reflections full of practical truths for believers. These meditations will draw out worship and marvel at the Lord's wonderful revelation of Jesus Christ and His work as prefigured in the Tabernacle. Illustrated.
ISBN 0-8254-3756-3   304 pp.   paper

**THE HOLY VESSELS AND FURNITURE
OF THE TABERNACLE**   **Henry W. Soltau**
A detailed delineation from Scritpure of the contents of the tabernacle. The furniture and vessels used in the tabernacle are all treated in their typical significance for the believer's instruction and practical application. 10 full-color illustrations.
ISBN 0-8254-3751-2   148 pp.   paper

**THE TABERNACLE, PRIESTHOOD,
AND THE OFFERINGS**   **Henry W. Soltau**
This exhaustive, richly suggestive treatment is a classic in its field. Charles H. Spurgeon evaluated this work by saying that it was "exceedingly well worked out in details, but not so wiredrawn as to prevent thought on the reader's part." Illustrated.
ISBN 0-8254-3750-4   496 pp.   paper

Available at your local Christian bookseller, or:

P. O. Box 2607 • Grand Rapids, MI 49501-2607